Money and Wealth as a Young Adult From the Ground Up

Master Essential Money Skills for Lifelong Financial Success

Victoria Rowan

Table of Contents

INTRODUCTION **6**

CHAPTER I: Understanding Money Basics **7**

Money Foundation 7

Personal Finance Basics 11

Building Money Confidence 17

Starting Your Financial Journey 22

CHAPTER II: Building Better Budgets **29**

Budget Foundations 29

Managing Monthly Money 33

Improving Budget Habits 39

Creating Your Spending Roadmap 44

CHAPTER III: Developing Saving Habits **52**

Savings Foundations 52

Emergency Savings 57

Growing Savings 62

Strengthening Your Financial Cushion 67

CHAPTER IV: Controlling Personal Debt **75**

Understanding Debt 75

Managing Debt 80

Avoiding Debt Problems 85

Moving Toward Financial Freedom 90

CHAPTER V: Increasing Your Income **98**

Growing Earning Power 98
Creating Extra Income 102
Improving Career Value 107
Professional Growth 113
CHAPTER VI: Starting Smart Investing 121
Investment Foundations 121
Choosing Investments 125
Building Investment Habits 130
Beginning Your Wealth Building 134
CHAPTER VII: Protecting Financial Progress 142
Understanding Financial Risk 142
Using Insurance 147
Building Financial Resilience 152
Creating Your Financial Safety Shield 157
CHAPTER VIII: Growing Long Term Wealth.................. 164
Understanding Wealth Creation 164
Building Multiple Assets 168
Maintaining Wealth Growth 172
Strengthening Your Wealth Foundation 177
CHAPTER IX: Planning Your Financial Future 184
Setting Financial Goals 184
Preparing Major Milestones 189
Reviewing Financial Progress 194
Designing Your Financial Roadmap 199

CHAPTER X: Creating Lasting Financial Success 206

Building Financial Discipline 206

Achieving Financial Independence 210

Creating A Lasting Legacy 214

Building Your Lifelong Financial Future 219

CONCLUSION 225

INTRODUCTION

The book Money and Wealth as a Young Adult From the Ground Up: Master Essential Money Skills for Lifelong Financial Success provides young individuals with the fundamental financial knowledge they need to create a secure and self-assured future. Making more money is not the only aspect of money management. It entails being aware of how daily decisions affect long-term security as well as spending, saving, budgeting, debt, investing, and financial objectives. Making intelligent decisions and avoiding costly mistakes gets easier the earlier these skills are mastered.

Significant financial opportunities and responsibilities come with young adulthood. Without a solid financial foundation, first employment, fluctuating income, educational costs, independent living, credit decisions, and future planning may easily become daunting. Early adoption of sound financial practices can increase control, lessen needless financial stress, and make it simpler to get ready for unforeseen obstacles. Consistently making small choices can develop into strong habits that have a long-term impact on financial advancement.

Those with great earnings or ideal conditions are not the only ones who can build wealth. It starts with awareness, self-control, tolerance, and a readiness to learn. Young individuals can progressively improve their financial situation by learning how money works and incorporating useful techniques into daily life. Developing enduring habits that promote freedom, opportunity, self-assurance, and increased control over the future is the aim.

CHAPTER I

Understanding Money Basics

Money Foundation

Understanding that financial success is not achieved by making a lot of money quickly is the first step toward building a solid financial foundation. It is developed through modest choices, dependable routines, and a thorough comprehension of the financial system. Early exposure to these concepts can have a big impact on a young adult's life. Almost all significant decisions, such as those pertaining to education, housing, transportation, relationships, career choices, travel, family duties, and future security, are influenced by money. Even a respectable income might rapidly vanish if one lacks financial literacy. Even a small income can serve as the foundation for stability and long-term growth if one has a solid understanding of finance. Therefore, understanding how to earn, manage, save, spend, protect, and develop money with purpose is essential to building a financial foundation.

Knowing where money comes from and how hard it takes to obtain it is the first step toward having a solid financial foundation. Employment, freelancing, company ventures, investments, and other legal sources can all provide income. Young adults frequently place a lot of emphasis on their income without taking into account how much of it is truly accessible after paying for necessities and other commitments. The amount that can be saved and invested is diminished by taxes, transportation, food, housing, bills, debt payments, and other expenses, even if gross income may appear spectacular. Increased awareness results from knowing the distinction between income and usable cash. Making decisions based on facts rather than conjecture is made easier by this insight.

Understanding the difference between needs and wants is another crucial component of financial strength. While wants are purchases that may offer pleasure, convenience, or status but are not required for survival or financial stability, needs are expenses that support fundamental life and obligations. Rejecting every pleasurable purchase is not the difference. Rather, it is about making deliberate decisions. Knowing this difference allows a young adult to enjoy life without letting short-term aspirations dictate long-term financial choices. It is helpful to consider if a purchase fulfills a significant obligation, advances a worthwhile objective, or merely satisfies an impulse before making a buy. Numerous needless expenses can be avoided with this easy habit.

Another crucial basis is provided by budgeting. A budget is neither a penalty nor a limitation. It is a strategy that clearly defines the purpose of money. Spending can become routine and challenging to manage without a budget. Paying bills, buying meals, using transportation, shopping online, hanging out with friends, and making modest everyday purchases can all be done without recognizing how quickly these costs add up. Visibility is produced with a straightforward budget. It displays the amount of money received, the amount spent on necessities, the amount that can be saved, and the amount left over for flexible spending. A budget that is reasonable enough to be regularly adhered to is the most beneficial. A simple plan that becomes a regular habit is more beneficial than a complex one that is dropped after a few weeks.

Additionally, saving needs to become a regular aspect of financial life rather than something that is only done when funds are available. Although many people put off saving money until the end of the month, spending frequently depletes what is left over. The pattern is altered when you pay yourself first. Before needless spending starts, a predetermined sum can be sent into savings as soon as income is received. The habit can be formed with even a tiny quantity. The amount saved might rise in tandem with income. The goal is to build financial flexibility rather than gain wealth. Savings can assist finance future objectives, offer support during unforeseen circumstances, and lessen the need to rely on debt when problems occur.

Young folks should especially have an emergency fund because unforeseen expenses can arise at any time. A financial plan may be disrupted by malfunctioning equipment, an urgent trip, a brief lack of income, essential house repairs, or other unforeseen costs. A person might have to take out a loan or use pricey credit if they don't have any savings. An emergency fund acts as a safety net between an unforeseen issue and a financial emergency. The process is easier to handle when it is built gradually. Individual circumstances, income stability, and essential costs will determine the required amount; however, it is crucial to start and maintain regular contributions.

Another important component of a sound financial foundation is debt management. While borrowing might occasionally assist someone in achieving significant objectives, debt also entails future responsibilities. Every loan must eventually be paid back, frequently with interest and other fees. Young individuals should be aware of how interest operates, how repayment timeframes are impacted by minimum payments, and how borrowing can limit future financial flexibility. When credit is used without considering its costs, it can lead to a vicious cycle where future income is consumed by current consumption. Knowing why money is being borrowed, comprehending the terms of repayment, and ensuring that the obligation fits into the overall financial plan are all components of responsible borrowing.

Organization of finances is equally important. Important documents should be kept safe and well-organized, including bank statements, bills, loan data, insurance paperwork, employment records, and account information. Errors, unauthorized transactions, forgotten subscriptions, and spending trends that require attention can all be found by routinely reviewing accounts. Additionally, financial organization facilitates decision-making by allowing one to view their actual financial situation instead of depending solely on recollection. A clear financial picture boosts self-assurance and lessens needless worry.

Learning to think beyond the here and now is also necessary for a solid foundation. Because time can be on their side, young adults have a significant edge. Early investments and savings have a greater chance of growing through compounding. This does not entail taking needless risks or hurrying into complex investments. It entails making it a habit to consider potential outcomes. A small amount saved regularly over a long period of time can have far greater significance than a large amount saved infrequently. Long-term planning promotes patience and lessens the pressure to amass wealth rapidly.

Rather than just reading about money, financial confidence is developed through activity. Making a budget, keeping track of spending, accumulating savings, making timely bill payments, cutting back on needless debt, learning about investing, and routinely evaluating progress all contribute to increased confidence. Errors may occur along the way, but when they are honestly analyzed, they can become important lessons. Financial perfection is not the aim. Consistent improvement is the aim. Each prudent financial choice builds on the one before it.

In the end, a financial foundation empowers young individuals to make more decisions. The ability to establish a business, assist loved ones, change occupations, complete education, deal with emergencies, and pursue important personal goals can all be made possible by financial security. Success is not determined by money alone. Gaining the knowledge and self-control to manage money sensibly is the bigger accomplishment. Young individuals are better equipped to establish stability before pursuing greater wealth when they are taught these concepts at a young age. A solid foundation transforms financial knowledge into everyday behavior, everyday behavior into long-lasting habits, and long-lasting habits into more future chances.

Personal Finance Basics

The first step in understanding the fundamentals of personal finance is to learn how to consciously handle money instead of letting it dictate everyday choices. This information is particularly crucial for young adults since early financial decisions can affect stability for many years to come. Having a large income is not the only aspect of personal finance. It entails being aware of how money is made, spent, borrowed, invested, saved, and safeguarded. If planning is lacking or spending is out of control, a person can make a significant amount of money yet still be under financial hardship. However, by forming disciplined habits and making deliberate decisions, a person with a little income can achieve significant progress. Therefore, the foundation of personal finance is not a person's wealth but rather their capacity for prudent resource management.

Understanding income is one of the first lessons. The money that can be obtained from employment, business ventures, freelance work, investments, or other legal sources is referred to as income. The difference between total earnings and the amount that is truly accessible for personal use after taxes, deductions, and mandatory contributions should be taught to young individuals. Financial planning becomes more feasible when take-home pay is understood. Additionally, it helps avoid the common error of basing expenditures on anticipated income rather than the actual funds that end up in a wallet or bank account. Every other financial decision is based on knowing precisely how much money is received each month.

Comprehending costs is equally crucial. Housing, food, transportation, utilities, education, communication, insurance, debt repayment, entertainment, personal expenditures, and other obligations are examples of expenses. While certain costs fluctuate from month to month, others are largely constant. Keeping track of spending can help identify trends that would otherwise be hard to spot. Even though small purchases might not seem like much on their own, they can add up to a significant amount of monthly cash. The purpose of keeping track of expenditures is not to instill anxiety. Rather, it gives information that enables an individual to determine if funds are being spent in accordance with personal priorities.

Income and spending are combined into a workable financial plan by budgeting. A budget enables an individual to make financial decisions before spending. Priority should be given to necessities, then savings, debt repayment, and personal expenditures. Depending on the specific situation, the structure can change. The plan's representation of actual revenue and reasonable expenses is crucial. A successful budget should be adaptable enough to accommodate common adjustments while yet safeguarding significant financial objectives. Financial decisions become more thoughtful and unforeseen shortfalls become less frequent when planning becomes a regular practice.

Another essential component of personal finance is saving. Saving money builds up a reserve that can be utilized for large obligations, future opportunities, planned purchases, education, travel, and emergencies. It's a prevalent misconception that one should start saving money only once they start making a lot of money. In actuality, the habit matters more than the initial quantity. Setting aside a tiny percentage of each pay check will help you develop self-control and establish a habit that you can stick to when your income rises. Because the money is sent before it is carelessly squandered, automatic transfers can facilitate saving. Regular saving can eventually grow small contributions into significant financial reserves.

An especially crucial type of protection is an emergency fund. Life is not always predictable financially. A person might have to pay for an unforeseen repair, medical care, a brief period of unemployment, an urgent family obligation, or another unavoidable expense. These circumstances may cause someone to borrow money or rely significantly on credit if they have no savings. During challenging times, an emergency reserve offers breathing room. The task can be less daunting if such a reserve is built gradually. To prevent one unforeseen incident from ruining months or years of progress, the objective is to build financial resilience.

Another important aspect of personal economics that young adults must comprehend is debt. While borrowing money might occasionally be helpful, each loan entails a future commitment. Interest implies that the amount repaid can exceed the initial loan amount. When utilized without a repayment plan, credit cards, personal loans, school loans, auto financing, and other types of borrowing can get costly. Understanding the interest rate, fees, payback schedule, minimum payment, and overall cost is crucial before taking on debt. When borrowing responsibly, one must consider the necessity of the purchase, the affordability of the payment, and the loan's impact on other financial objectives.

Because credit history might affect future financial possibilities, credit management requires careful consideration. Responsible credit behavior can be supported by making timely payments, controlling borrowing, and examining financial statements. While bad credit practices can result in extra expenses and restrictions, a good credit record may make it simpler to apply for some financial products under favorable circumstances. Therefore, rather than viewing credit as more money, young adults should view it as a financial obligation. Although credit makes it possible to borrow money, it does not actually enhance wealth, only because it makes more money available for expenditure.

Safeguarding funds and private data is a crucial component of personal finance. Payment cards, bank accounts, passwords, identification documents, and financial information should all be handled with caution. Finding odd transactions or errors might be aided by routinely reviewing account activity. Fraud vulnerability can be reduced by using strong passwords, secure authentication techniques, and vigilance when handling unknown financial messages. Increasing wealth is not the sole way to achieve financial security. Preventing avoidable losses is another aspect of it. A person who puts a lot of effort into saving money should take sensible precautions to safeguard those funds.

Goal-setting is equally necessary for personal finance. Without objectives, budgeting and saving can feel more like constraints than worthwhile endeavors. Money has a purpose when it has a financial objective. Building savings or paying off a specific debt are examples of short-term objectives. Education, housing, transportation, or launching a business are examples of medium-term objectives. Retirement, investment development, financial freedom, and fulfilling family obligations are examples of long-term objectives. When goals are practical, quantifiable, time-bound, and detailed, they become more valuable. Setting clear goals helps people determine which financial decisions should be prioritized.

Investing becomes a crucial topic to comprehend when financial stability increases. Investing carries risk, but it can also offer chances for money to increase over time. Before making financial decisions, young adults should get familiar with fundamental ideas including diversification, time horizon, fees, risk tolerance, and compound growth. Investing shouldn't be viewed as a quick way to become wealthy. It is better viewed as a lengthy process that calls for perseverance, investigation, and sensible risk management. There may be more opportunities for disciplined contributions and long-term growth to coexist if strong investment habits are established early.

Understanding lifestyle choices is another aspect of personal finance. There may be pressure to raise expenditure at the same rate as income. Lifestyle inflation is another term for this. A raise may be used to upgrade housing, transportation, clothes, entertainment, or other expenses right away, leaving little extra cash for investments or savings. Allowing income growth to enhance both current quality of life and future financial security is a better strategy. While it makes sense to enjoy increased income, keeping some of the prior expenditure level can free up more space for debt reduction, investing, and saving.

Additionally, financial education ought to be seen as a continuous process. Financial goods, the state of the economy, job prospects, technology, and individual situations are all subject to change. A person who keeps learning is more equipped to adjust. Regular financial habits include reviewing a budget, monitoring savings progress, assessing debt, learning about investment possibilities, and modifying goals. Instead of being a reason to give up on financial planning, mistakes should be viewed as chances for improvement. Every financial choice reveals what is effective and what needs to be altered.

In the end, developing control, flexibility, and confidence is what personal finance fundamentals are all about. The objective is not to live in perpetual limitation or to forgo every pleasurable purchase. The objective is to understand the effects of financial actions and make decisions that meet both current needs and future priorities. Money becomes a helpful tool rather than a continual cause of worry when income is carefully handled, spending is tracked, savings are accumulated, debt is managed, credit is used appropriately, and long-term goals are persistently pursued. Young adult behaviors can last for decades, impacting opportunities, financial freedom, job choices, and family responsibilities.

Early acquisition of these concepts offers a useful basis for making better choices and creating a more secure future.

Building Money Confidence

Developing the conviction that financial abilities can be acquired, exercised, and enhanced is the first step in building financial confidence. Because they have never been taught how to manage spending, understand credit, make investment decisions, develop a budget, or save consistently, many young adults feel uneasy when it comes to money. Avoidance, rash judgments, or reliance on others to make financial decisions might result from this uncertainty. Having complete financial knowledge or never making mistakes are not prerequisites for having financial confidence. It entails developing an open mind, asking questions, looking over financial data, and making deliberate choices based on individual circumstances and objectives. When knowledge is paired with consistent action, confidence increases.

Understanding your existing financial condition is one of the most crucial stages toward financial confidence. Without knowledge of earnings, expenses, obligations, and savings, one cannot handle money with confidence. It may be unsettling to look at these figures at first, particularly if debt has grown or spending has been out of control. Avoiding financial knowledge, however, doesn't make things better. Making improvements is made possible by awareness. Financial decisions become less enigmatic and easier to handle when income, expenses, savings, and commitments are all fully known. A person starts substituting information for uncertainty.

One useful method to cultivate this awareness is to keep track of your spending. Every purchase reveals details about a person's priorities and behaviors. Spending on food, travel, entertainment, subscriptions, internet shopping, and other activities on a regular basis might highlight trends that might not be apparent when looking at individual transactions. The goal of keeping track of spending is not to induce guilt. Rather, it enables one to observe where money is truly flowing and assess whether expenditure aligns with significant objectives. Instead of speculating about what needs to change, young adults can make changes with more certainty when they are aware of their spending habits.

Because it gives one direction, budgeting also boosts financial confidence. A budget offers a strategy for allocating income based on priorities. One can allocate funds to necessary expenses, savings, debt repayment, and flexible spending rather than worrying about whether there will be enough for future expenses. The budget turns into a financial road plan that facilitates decision-making. It also offers a means of gauging advancement. A person's confidence starts to grow once they successfully stick to a budget for a few weeks or months since they have proof that financial discipline is achievable.

Another effective practice for boosting confidence is saving on a regular basis. Even if a person may start off little, regular saving can have a big psychological impact. Every donation shows that funds can be purposefully saved rather than wasted right away. The person feels more secure and in control as the balance increases. Eventually, savings can help with investing objectives, future purchases, schooling, professional prospects, and emergencies. More significantly, saving cultivates the habit of seeing beyond short-term needs. It instills patience and reaffirms the idea that modest efforts taken repeatedly over time can yield significant outcomes.

When someone learns to deal with mistakes in a productive way, financial confidence also grows. Almost everyone makes financial choices that they come to regret. Spending excessively, taking on needless debt, forgetting a bill, making an inappropriate purchase, or failing to save at an opportunity to do so are all possible. Ignoring or repeating an error makes it more harmful. Examining what went wrong, figuring out why it happened, and figuring out what can be done differently the next time is a confident attitude. Errors are turned into lessons by this process. Financial maturity is determined by improving one's ability to identify and remedy bad actions rather than by having a flawless record.

Financial worry can also be lessened by understanding debt. When a borrower is unaware of how interest, repayment terms, and minimum payments operate, debt frequently feels overwhelming. Acquiring these facts can help you manage your debt. A person has greater control than someone who doesn't check the account if they are aware of the balance, interest rate, required payments, and repayment plan. The situation can be gradually improved by prioritizing costlier debt, avoiding needless new borrowing, and paying more than the minimum when financially feasible. Each successful payment can boost self-esteem and show that advancement is achievable.

Another area where knowledge can take the place of uncertainty is credit. Young individuals should be aware that credit is borrowed funds, not more money. Paying bills on time, managing balances, checking statements, and being aware of borrowing charges are all components of responsible credit utilization. There is less incentive to treat available credit as unrestricted spending power when one is aware of how credit operates. This information can lessen the chance of accruing costly debt and save future financial prospects.

Learning to make decisions on your own is also necessary for financial confidence. Spending and investment decisions can be influenced by friends, advertisements, social media, family, and financial influencers. Personal financial decisions should ultimately be based on individual goals, income, responsibilities, risk tolerance, and circumstances, but their advice may occasionally be helpful. A self-assured individual is able to hear advice without necessarily acting on it. Rather, before acting, the individual looks for trustworthy information, weighs possible outcomes, and asks whether the advice makes sense. When making financial judgments involving large sums of money, independent thot is particularly crucial.

Learning to distinguish one's financial identity from one's financial situation is a crucial component of confidence. A person is not incapable of achieving financial success if they have a low salary, few savings, or debt. Education, professional growth, frugal spending, saving, and careful planning can all improve one's financial situation. A challenging financial beginning should be seen as an opportunity for improvement rather than a long-term indicator of one's value. This kind of thinking makes it easier to concentrate on workable answers and promotes action rather than shame.

Financial confidence can also be enhanced by raising income. While controlling current finances is crucial, acquiring useful skills might increase earning potential in the future. Opportunities for increased income may arise from education, professional certifications, technical proficiency, leadership, communication skills, entrepreneurship, and specialized knowledge. However, when combined with sound financial practices, higher earnings become more valuable. Income growth may not result in long-term improvement if every raise is quickly swallowed by increased spending. Knowing how to use extra money wisely by boosting savings, cutting debt, investing, and enhancing quality of life in balanced ways gives you confidence.

When objectives are well-defined, financial confidence increases. When money is linked to something worthwhile, it is simpler to maintain motivation. Building an emergency fund, paying off debt, buying a house, helping family members, starting a business, going back to school, traveling, or getting ready for retirement are all possible goals. Financial discipline has a purpose thanks to goals. Additionally, they facilitate the process of determining what has to be addressed today. When compared to a significant long-term goal, a purchase that initially sounds desirable may lose its attraction.

Patience is also necessary for long-term confidence. It is rare for financial advancement to occur immediately. Investments may change over time, savings may increase slowly, and debt may take months or years to pay off. Comparing one's own development to the seeming success of others might lead to needless frustration. Social media frequently displays accomplishments and belongings without disclosing the debt, family support, income, or financial situation that led to them. Measuring development in relation to personal objectives is a healthy strategy. Every saved sum, lowered debt, avoided pointless purchases, finished financial lesson, and enhanced habit signifies progress in the right direction.

In the end, developing financial confidence is a process of transforming doubt into comprehension and comprehension into action. It is not necessary for a young adult to become an expert in finance before taking charge of their finances. Simple steps like keeping track of spending, making a realistic budget, saving frequently, paying bills on time, learning about credit, cutting back on needless debt, and establishing worthwhile financial objectives can start the process. Confidence develops organically as these behaviors become routines. The individual starts to have confidence in their capacity to make choices, handle financial difficulties, and adapt to changing conditions. Money confidence offers more than just financial literacy. It gives people a sense of control that can affect their future plans, relationships, career choices, and prospects. Money becomes less daunting and more helpful as a tool for establishing stability, independence, and long-term opportunity when financial confidence is gradually developed and backed by appropriate practices.

Starting Your Financial Journey

Being financially capable starts with realizing how important money is. When awareness turns into action, the true transformation takes place. A young adult can transition from reacting to money to purposefully managing it by knowing what money is, how it affects daily actions, and the repercussions of financial choices. This is important since early adulthood financial habits have a lasting impact. When responsibilities grow, a person who learns to monitor income, expenses, priorities, and financial behavior is better equipped to make deliberate judgments. Even a small income can serve as a helpful foundation for saving, handling responsibilities, becoming ready for crises, and creating future opportunities when this awareness is applied consistently. Without this knowledge, money can quickly vanish due to impulsive spending, emotional choices, needless borrowing, and behaviors that are hard to see until they cause major issues.

In everyday circumstances, the distinction between financial awareness and financial negligence can be seen. Think about two young individuals who make the same amount of money each month. The first person makes purchases without considering where the money is going. Because each individual expense seems reasonable, small purchases appear innocuous. But there isn't much money left at the end of the month. The person may have to borrow money if an unforeseen expense arises because they have no reserves. The second person keeps an eye on spending trends and determines ahead of time how much can be allocated to future wants, personal fun, and essentials. Although the money has a more obvious purpose, this person does not necessarily make more money. There is a greater likelihood of having something ready to deal with an unforeseen expense. Income is not the key distinction. It is consciousness followed by purposeful action.

More than just a bank balance can be altered by using financial understanding. It can alter a young adult's perspective on money. Understanding can progressively replace confusion. Anxiety may turn into preparation. Intentional expenditure can develop from impulsive spending. Financial helplessness can transform into a sense of control. Relationships, employment, education, housing, and personal freedom can all be impacted by these shifts. A person who is aware of their financial situation would be less inclined to take on an inappropriate financial commitment just because it appears reasonable right now. Additionally, because they are more aware of what they can actually afford, they can be more eager to seize opportunities.

Neglecting financial literacy might have the opposite impact. Because they go unrecognized, minor issues can grow into major ones. Because money is uncomfortable, a person may continue to spend a little bit more than is necessary, frequently use credit for routine purchases, put off saving money, or avoid having financial conversations. None of these choices always result in an emergency. Repetitive decisions run the risk of becoming patterns. A person's financial future may be impacted by patterns that develop into habits. Financial problems frequently don't show up overnight. They can progressively emerge from numerous common choices that were never really considered.

The straightforward practice of assessing spending at the end of each week provides a useful illustration. Consider a young worker who thinks that the majority of their regular revenue is used for necessities. The employee finds that a significant amount of revenue is being consumed by a number of tiny meal deliveries, convenience purchases, entertainment costs, and pointless memberships after keeping track of every purchase for four weeks. Eliminating all pleasurable activities is not necessary for the discovery. Rather, the employee selects two costs to cut and puts that money into savings. Although the change is slight, it illustrates a crucial idea. Seeing what is already happening clearly is frequently the first step toward improving one's financial situation rather than making a significantly higher salary.

This concept is demonstrated in a short narrative. Anna, a young lady, was pleased to be able to handle her own finances after receiving her first regular income. She thot she could always make more money later, so she spent freely throughout the first few months. She occasionally borrowed money from acquaintances before payday, paid for meals without considering the cost, and purchased items she desired. Her phone required an unforeseen repair after a month. She couldn't afford it because she didn't have any savings. She learned from that experience that becoming financially independent involved more than just earning money. She started keeping track of her expenses, allocating a tiny portion of each pay check, and evaluating her decisions every week. A few months later, there was still another unforeseen cost. She was ready this time. She didn't have a lot of money saved, but it was plenty to handle the issue without taking out a loan. Her income did not alter. Her consciousness and actions were altered.

Considering financial understanding as a compass is a helpful metaphor. A person cannot be guided toward a goal by a compass alone. It just makes the direction more apparent. Similarly, wealth is not immediately created by understanding how money is made, spent, saved, and managed. It offers the data required to make a better decision. A tourist can move farther away from their intended location while walking confidently without a compass. A person who lacks financial literacy may also make self-assured choices that progressively erode their independence and security. Direction is provided by awareness, and progress is produced by constant activity.

By the end of this chapter, you will be able to determine which financial habits have the biggest impact on your day-to-day choices, assess whether the way you currently manage your finances meets your immediate needs and long-term goals, and develop a straightforward personal system for monitoring and enhancing your financial behavior. Because financial capacity is developed through experience rather than memorization of financial words, these results are valuable. Becoming flawless with money is not the aim. Increasing intentionality is the aim. You are improving your financial judgment each time you consider a purchase before making it, identify a needless spend, make a tiny save, or consider whether a financial choice aligns with your values.

This lesson can be applied right away using a straightforward structure known as the See Choose Act Review technique. The first stage is to have a thorough understanding of your existing circumstances. Examine your recent earnings and expenses without passing judgment on yourself. Instead of writing down what you think happened, write down what actually happened. Selecting one area that needs improvement is the second stage. Don't try to make all the changes at once. Pick one action that can have a significant impact, such as cutting back on pointless purchases or saving money as soon as you get paid. Taking action on that choice is the third step. Make the modification realistic and targeted. Rather than promising to cut back on spending, make a commitment to cut back on a specific needless expense or to put a certain amount into savings each time you get paid. Reviewing the outcome is the fourth phase. Examine the changes after a few days or weeks. Proceed with the choice if it was successful. If it didn't work, figure out why and modify the strategy. A cycle of awareness, decision-making, action, and improvement is thus created.

Because it keeps financial awareness from turning into passive observation, the See Choose Act Review technique is helpful. Many people are aware that they should practice better money management, but doing and knowing are two different things. Information is obtained through seeing. Making a decision results in intention. Movement is produced by acting. Learning is produced by reviewing. When combined, these actions make financial literacy a useful habit. This framework can be used by a young adult while examining spending, before making a significant purchase, after receiving a pay check, or whenever their financial situation changes.

A silent financial check might be used to start an immediate application. Ask yourself how much of your available funds are already being used for essential needs. Next, look at your previous expenditures and pick one habit or purchase that doesn't really align with your priorities. Next, choose one little financial task that you can finish today. It might be putting a little money into savings, terminating a service that isn't being used, keeping track of spending, examining a financial commitment, or setting a straightforward spending cap. The action should be realistic enough for you to be able to finish it. The goal is not to build a flawless financial system overnight. The goal is to demonstrate to yourself that one deliberate choice can start the process of improving your financial situation.

Anytime your financial circumstances change, you can apply the same strategy. A new job, higher or lower income, graduation, moving, taking on new responsibilities, or making a significant purchase can all alter how money should be handled. Take a moment to reflect rather than automatically carrying on with old routines. Inquire about what has changed, what is still significant, and how this should affect financial behavior. Because financial life is ever-changing, this flexibility is crucial. A tactic that is effective at one stage of adulthood might need to be modified in another.

Honesty is also necessary for financial awareness. It is simple to concentrate on financial data that gives you comfort while ignoring data that indicates issues. One may proudly keep track of their earnings yet refrain from looking at their debt. Someone else might prioritize saving money while disregarding wasteful spending. Someone else might be fully aware of the amount of money in an account, but they might not be aware of the amount needed to fulfill future commitments. To be truly aware, one must consider the whole picture. It entails being prepared to acknowledge one's strengths and shortcomings without letting shame or fear stop one from taking action.

This last piece is not meant to promote continual financial anxiety. Rather than causing ongoing tension, sound financial awareness should lead to more tranquility. You can make more confident selections when you are aware of your financial situation. You can tell the difference between a transient desire and a real financial constraint. You are able to distinguish between opportunities that are affordable and those that are likely to put undue pressure on you. Because you have quantifiable proof that your conduct is getting better, you can also celebrate your improvement.

Thus, you should incorporate reflection into your daily financial regimen. Which financial habit presently works best for you, and how might it be strengthened? Which spending habits put the biggest barrier in the way of your financial objectives? What recent financial choice would you make differently now? What modest step can you take to improve your financial awareness this week? What kind of financial life do you hope your current behaviors will lead to in the future?

It's not necessary to have a lot of cash, a high income, or flawless understanding to begin a financial adventure. Paying attention is the first step. You can start making smarter decisions after you have a comprehensive understanding of your financial behavior. Stronger habits are formed when better decisions are made repeatedly. Increased stability, adaptability, and opportunity can result from stronger habits. The most crucial lesson is that those with money are not the only ones who can advance financially. It can start with the individual who chooses to comprehend their finances, accept accountability for their decisions, and make one beneficial change at a time. Your financial future is influenced not just by your income but also by the purposeful use of what you already have.

CHAPTER II

Building Better Budgets

Budget Foundations

One of the most crucial pillars of financial stability is budgeting since it provides a clear picture of where money comes from and departs. Learning to make and stick to a budget is more than just cutting expenses for a young adult. It involves raising awareness, making deliberate choices, and building a financial framework that meets both immediate needs and long-term objectives. Without a budget, it's simple to spend money without understanding how quickly little purchases add up. After receiving a pay check, paying a few obvious bills, and making a few sporadic purchases, one may question why there isn't much left. By making money management a conscious endeavor, a budget alters this pattern. It offers a straightforward framework for determining what should be prioritized and what may wait.

Understanding actual revenue is the first step toward creating a solid budget. Young adults can get money from commissions, freelance work, jobs, business ventures, allowances, and other sources. Working with actual amounts instead of optimistic assumptions is crucial. It is useful to estimate using a cautious amount based on consistent earnings if income fluctuates from month to month. Since the amount paid before taxes and deductions is not always the amount accessible for daily expenses, it is particularly crucial to understand take-home pay. Expenses can be compared to real available revenue once it is known. This straightforward comparison serves as the foundation for assessing the sustainability of financial practices.

Understanding costs is the next pillar. Needs, wants, savings, and financial commitments are common categories for expenses. Food, housing, utilities, transportation, communication, and basic personal care are examples of essentials. Entertainment, eating out, hobbies, subscriptions, shopping, and other discretionary purchases are examples of wants. Debt repayment, insurance, tuition, and family responsibilities are examples of financial obligations. Savings are funds that are purposefully set aside for future needs and objectives. These classifications assist young individuals in realizing that not all costs are equally high. Budgeting does not mean sacrificing enjoyment. Rather, it aids in striking a balance between covering essential costs and keeping discretionary spending within acceptable bounds.

Differentiating between fixed and variable expenses is a crucial component of budget foundations. Rent, loan payments, and some subscriptions are examples of fixed expenses that are often pretty constant each month. Groceries, transportation, entertainment, clothing, and eating out are examples of variable expenses that can vary based on behavior and circumstances. Understanding this distinction makes it simpler to determine where changes can be made when finances get tight. While a person might not be able to lower a fixed housing payment quickly, they might be able to change how much they spend on entertainment, dining out, or shopping. Instead of having a budget feel like a harsh set of limitations, this knowledge allows it flexibility.

Instead of regarding saves as whatever is left over at the end of the month, a functional budget should include savings as a deliberate component of the plan. There can be little or nothing left to save if saving is put off until after all expenses have been made. A stronger habit is formed when a certain amount is set away each time income is received. When saved regularly, even a small sum can have significance. Emergencies, education, large purchases, travel, personal growth, and long-term financial objectives are just a few of the uses for savings. The most crucial lesson is that saving money should become a habit rather than a sporadic choice.

Budgeting also emphasizes the value of being ready for unforeseen costs. Even though some expenses don't show up every month, they can still put a lot of strain on finances. Ignoring annual fees, school bills, gifts, car maintenance, medical demands, home repairs, or seasonal purchases all cause budget disruptions. Anticipating these costs and progressively allocating funds for them is a more effective strategy. This approach turns unforeseen financial strain into planned financial accountability. Many ostensibly unforeseen expenses are actually predictable when considered over a longer period of time, even though not every emergency can be forecast.

The ability to identify spending trends is one of budgeting's biggest advantages. Even if a person might think that sporadic purchases don't have much of an impact, looking across a few weeks or months' worth of transactions can highlight significant patterns. When small purchases are made repeatedly, they might grow to be significant. Convenience purchases, impulsive buying, frequent meal delivery, unused subscriptions, and pointless fees can all silently deplete funds that could be utilized for savings or other crucial objectives. Examining these trends is not meant to incite guilt. Its purpose is to raise awareness. It is simpler to determine if a spending behavior should persist, alter, or cease once it becomes apparent.

A budget ought to be reasonable as well. Although it may seem impressive on paper, creating a very limited plan might be challenging to implement in real life. A person may eventually give up on a budget if it does not allow for acceptable enjoyment, unforeseen expenses, or shifting circumstances. A sustainable budget acknowledges that life involves both obligations and individual decisions. Consistency, not perfection, is the aim. A person who makes a flawless budget for a week and then gives up is unlikely to make as much progress financially as someone who adheres to a fair budget for several months.

When budgeting is linked to certain financial objectives, it becomes even more effective. It can be challenging to save money without understanding why, particularly when instant purchases appear more alluring. Savings have meaning when they have a goal. A young adult may wish to establish a business, start an emergency fund, buy a car, pay for schooling, move into a new house, or start investing for the future. The budget can allocate funds toward the goal once it has been established. As a result, budgeting becomes a system of direction rather than a system of limitations. Every financial choice can be assessed by determining if it strengthens or undermines the most important priorities.

Budgeting can also be made simpler by technology. Spreadsheets, automatic transfers, banking apps, and financial tracking tools can all lessen the work involved in keeping an eye on finances. Technology, however, cannot take the place of sound financial management. Even with the most sophisticated budgeting software, someone might still make bad choices if they don't keep an honest eye on their expenditures. Only when precise data is entered and the resulting plan is adhered to is the tool beneficial. When applied consistently, simple techniques can be just as successful as complex systems.

Building a relationship with money based on awareness, accountability, and purpose is the ultimate goal of budget foundations. Instead of depending solely on speculation, a budget enables young individuals to view their financial reality clearly. It helps avoid overspending, improves saving behaviors, prepares for unforeseen expenses, and paves the road for significant financial objectives. Financial decisions become less stressful when budgeting becomes a regular part of life since there is a strategy in place. Many subsequent decisions, such as borrowing, investing, housing, career choices, and long-term wealth creation, can be influenced by the habits formed by budgeting. Seldom does a solid financial future start with a lot of money. The ability to handle the money that is already accessible is generally the first step. Thus, developing a sound budget is one of the most useful ways to achieve financial independence, self-assurance, and long-term stability.

Managing Monthly Money

One of the most useful skills a young adult can acquire is monthly money management since it transforms income into a clear strategy for fulfilling obligations, limiting spending, accumulating savings, and planning for future requirements. A fresh cycle of earnings and outlays occurs every month, and how that cycle is handled can have a long-term impact on financial stability. Making money is just one aspect of being financially successful. Additionally, one must know how much money is accessible, when it will arrive, where it must go, and how much can be used for personal decisions without risk. Without a strategy, little purchases and unforeseen costs can quickly deplete funds. Even a small income can be better managed and allocated to key goals with a consistent strategy.

Understanding the amount of revenue that can be used is the first step in managing monthly finances. A young adult may be supported financially by family, earnings from part-time employment, freelancing payments, business income, or a salary. The amount received might not always be the same each month, especially if revenue varies based on business activity or working hours. Instead of presuming that the best potential income will continue continuously, it is crucial to deal with actual numbers. Planning around a conservative estimate can offer more security when income fluctuates. Instead of being immediately incorporated into regular expenditure, any additional income can then be put toward savings, debt reduction, future objectives, or other beneficial uses.

Finding regular expenses is the next step after comprehending income. Housing, utilities, food, transportation, communication, education, insurance, debt repayment, and other essential responsibilities are a few examples. While some costs fluctuate based on consumption or other factors, others are largely constant each month. Financial planning is made simpler by keeping fixed and variable spending apart. Flexible costs can be changed, whereas fixed expenses typically need to be paid regardless of spending decisions. When money gets tight, knowing this gap makes it easier to see where changes can be made. Flexible expenses are frequently easier to cut than necessary commitments in the event of an unexpected drop in income.

Every percentage of revenue has a function when it is part of a monthly spending plan. One can determine ahead of time how much should go toward needs, savings, debt repayment, personal expenditures, and future objectives rather than spending first and attempting to save what's left. This does not imply that every peso needs to be allocated precisely. A good plan should be adaptable and realistic. Creating awareness and direction is the aim. Frustration may result in giving up on the plan entirely if it is so restrictive that it cannot be followed. A sensible budget ensures that significant obligations are safeguarded while permitting everyday enjoyment.

Keeping track of actual spending is one of the most beneficial practices. While cost tracking reveals actual spending, a planned budget reveals intended spending. It is helpful to compare the two. Someone may find that food purchases have gone up, that transportation expenses are higher than anticipated, or that a number of minor internet purchases are costing a substantial quantity of money. The next month may see changes as a result of these findings. Finding trends is more important than criticizing every buy. When decisions are made using actual data rather than conjecture, financial management improves.

Controlling impulsive spending is another aspect of managing monthly finances. The goal of modern shopping is to make spending easy. Online retailers, digital payment methods, special offers, subscriptions, and ads might persuade consumers to make purchases before determining if they are necessary. Establishing a brief waiting period before making unnecessary purchases is a helpful practice. The pause gives you time to think about whether the purchase was planned, whether it fits the budget, and whether the funds could be better spent somewhere else. Many purchases that could later cause regret can be avoided with this easy approach.

Another area where managing monthly finances might be challenging is food expenditures. A significant amount of revenue can be gradually consumed by eating out, ordering delivery, buying snacks regularly, and making impromptu supermarket visits. This does not imply that eating out or consuming fast food must be avoided. Alternatively, the monthly plan may purposefully incorporate these options. Costs can be managed by preparing meals when feasible, creating shopping lists, comparing prices, and avoiding pointless purchases. Over time, modest adjustments to regular food expenditures can result in significant savings.

Careful consideration should also be given to transportation. High monthly costs can result from regular commuting, fuel, maintenance, fares, parking, and sporadic repairs. Instead of concentrating solely on the current cost of a car or journey, one should take the entire cost of transportation into account. When gasoline, maintenance, insurance, and other expenses are taken into account, a transportation option that initially seems inexpensive may turn out to be costly. It is possible to avoid transportation costs interfering with other financial objectives by planning them ahead of time.

Paying payments on time is a crucial component of monthly money management. Late payments can result in penalties, harm credit records, and needless anxiety. The likelihood of forgetting a commitment can be decreased by keeping a calendar of due dates or, when suitable, utilizing automatic payments. However, you should only use automated payments when you have enough money. Being financially organized entails being aware of both what must be paid and when funds will be available to pay for it. Timing is important because if multiple significant payments are made before the next income comes in, even someone with a sufficient monthly income may have difficulties.

Instead of being a voluntary activity, savings should be viewed as a regular monthly obligation. Consistent saving becomes a habit and eventually provides financial security, even if the amount is modest. Depending on their unique situation, young adults might set up a variety of savings goals. A fraction may be set aside for a short-term purpose, another for longer-term goals, and a third for emergency requirements. It can be easier to understand progress if savings are broken down by purpose. There might be less of an incentive to spend money carelessly when it has a purpose.

Monthly budgeting must also account for debt payments. The necessary payment should be seen as an essential requirement when there is debt. If at all possible, making extra payments on expensive debt can hasten development and lower interest costs in the future. Repaying debt, however, should be balanced with storing at least some money for emergencies and keeping enough cash on hand for necessities. Aggressive debt repayment without a cash reserve can lead to a scenario where a minor emergency necessitates additional borrowing. Both short-term stability and long-term debt reduction are taken into account in a balanced plan.

When financial objectives are linked to daily choices, managing monthly finances becomes simpler. Building an emergency fund, paying for schooling, starting a business, buying a house, traveling, or making investments for the future are all possible goals. When compared to big sums of money, these objectives may appear far off. They are easier to manage when divided into monthly contributions. One might concentrate on the next contribution rather than just the total. Every month becomes a chance to get a little bit closer to the intended outcome.

Regularly reviewing the monthly plan is also crucial. Financial conditions fluctuate. Rent may go up, income may go down, transportation needs may shift, debt may be settled, or new obligations may arise. A budget that was effective a few months ago might not be appropriate now. Examining the strategy enables one to make changes before issues worsen. This procedure should not be seen as proof that the initial strategy was unsuccessful, but rather as routine financial upkeep. Since real life is ever-changing, effective money management necessitates flexibility.

It may be made much simpler with a straightforward monthly schedule. Income and anticipated expenses can be examined at the start of each month. It is possible to organize debt payments, identify essential payments, designate savings, and set aside a fair amount for flexible spending. Actual spending can be tracked during the month. Spending can be examined near the end of the month to see what worked and what needs to be adjusted. This results in an ongoing cycle of preparation, action, evaluation, and enhancement. With time, the procedure becomes second nature and needs less work.

In the end, monthly money management offers more than just budgetary control. It lowers uncertainty and raises financial awareness. Financial decisions are easier to make when one is aware of their earnings, debts, expenses, savings, and goals. A person who can successfully manage a month is also better equipped to handle more responsibility in the future. Establishing fundamental monthly money management skills makes it easier to manage housing, family costs, investments, business decisions, and long-term financial commitments.

The most crucial lesson is that regular judgments made over time typically result in financial advancement. A flawless income or an intricate financial structure are not prerequisites for starting. They require alertness, discipline, consistency, and a readiness to adapt. A young adult can establish a solid financial routine by organizing expenditures, limiting wasteful spending, safeguarding funds, making timely payments, and routinely analyzing outcomes. Managing monthly finances helps provide the steadiness required for more ambitious financial objectives and transforms revenue into meaningful action. Money becomes simpler to comprehend and manage when these routines are incorporated into daily life, enabling each month to contribute to increased self-assurance, independence, and long-term financial security.

Improving Budget Habits

Young adults can have more control over their finances and make confident financial decisions by continuously improving their budgeting practices. When a budget is realistic, it can be helpful, but how well it works relies on the behaviors that surround it. Seldom do long-term outcomes occur from creating a budget once and then forgetting about it. Regular attention, honest assessment, correction, and consistency all contribute to the development of sound financial habits. Developing better budgeting practices does not include being fixated on every little purchase or refusing to spend money on pleasurable activities. It entails knowing how to allocate funds to the most important things while cutting waste and avoiding choices that put undue strain on finances.

Establishing a regular strategy for monitoring income and expenses is one of the first stages to changing budget habits. Because they are afraid of finding out they have spent more than they had anticipated, many people avoid closely examining their finances. But avoiding the numbers doesn't solve the issue. Frequent financial reviews offer helpful data that can help make smarter choices. Every week, a young adult can choose a certain day to analyze recent purchases, impending payments, savings progress, and remaining spending funds. This practice raises awareness before issues worsen. The individual may see what has to be changed while there is still time to react, as opposed to realizing at the end of the month that money is gone.

Learning to distinguish between required and impulsive or emotional expenditure is another significant development. Not all purchases are made because they are truly necessary. Boredom, stress, social pressure, convenience, or the need for instant gratification can all lead to purchasing. Budgeting can be far more successful when the emotional motivations for spending are acknowledged. Before making a non-essential purchase, a person should think about whether the item is really necessary, whether it fits within their present budget, and whether the purchase advances a significant objective. Many needless expenses can be avoided by taking this brief break. Intentional spending becomes more natural over time when deliberate decision-making is practiced.

Setting reasonable spending boundaries is another necessary step in improving budgeting practices. A budget should offer sufficient structure to safeguard financial priorities without becoming overly restrictive. A person may become frustrated and give up on the budgeting method altogether if they consistently go over unreasonable boundaries. Studying real spending trends and setting sensible limits is a superior strategy. If a particular amount is consistently spent on food, transportation, entertainment, or personal expenses, the budget should be realistic while yet pointing out areas that could be improved. Dramatic reductions are frequently less sustainable than gradual decreases. Gradually cutting back on wasteful expenditure can produce long-lasting benefits without making day-to-day living unduly challenging.

Preparing purchases in advance is another beneficial practice. Unplanned spending frequently happens when someone doesn't think about how a purchase will impact the remainder of the month. Impulse buying can be decreased by preparing a shopping list, comparing prices, postponing unnecessary purchases, and establishing a spending cap before going into a store or placing an online order. Additionally, planning facilitates the identification of marketing strategies that push consumers to spend more than they had planned. If the item was never needed in the first place, a discount does not result in savings. When someone spends less on something that was already required or purposefully planned, they are truly saving money.

Budgeting practices can be strengthened even further by automation. Shortly after income is received, regular automated transfers can shift funds to savings, lessening the incentive to spend them. When utilized sensibly and with enough money, automatic bill payments can also assist in avoiding missed deadlines and late fines. Automation can make healthy habits easier to sustain, but it does not eliminate the need for financial literacy. Positive financial behaviors become ingrained in a person's habits when they occur regularly and don't require a fresh choice each month.

Being ready for unforeseen expenses is another aspect of having a solid budget. Many people make budgets based solely on monthly payments and daily expenses, only to become irritated when yearly or infrequent expenses show up. If they are neglected, expenses for school, birthdays, vacations, maintenance, medical needs, holidays, or yearly subscriptions can cause financial plans to fall apart. In order to improve a budget, one must look beyond the current month and discover potential future expenses. It can be easier to manage these expenses when they come up if you set aside little sums on a regular basis. This strategy lessens the need to borrow money or rely on credit if an unforeseen need arises.

Improving budgeting practices should also include debt management. Paying off debt should not be viewed as optional costs but rather as significant financial obligations. An account may remain current if only the minimal amount is paid, but interest can increase the cost of debt over time. When feasible, a careful budget can find ways to increase payments while preserving necessary savings. Preventing needless additional debt is similarly crucial. Before taking out a loan, one should think about whether the purchase is essential, whether the repayment would fit comfortably into future earnings, and how the debt might impact other financial objectives.

Learning from mistakes rather than letting them discourage you is another way to improve your spending habits. Almost everyone ultimately goes over budget, forgets to pay a bill, buys something needless, or underestimates a cost. A single error does not indicate a failure in budgeting. Analyzing what transpired and determining what may be altered are crucial. If the lack of a limit on entertainment led to excessive spending, a more explicit limit may be established. A reminder or automatic payment could be helpful if a bill were overlooked. Increasing the size of your emergency fund could be the answer if an emergency causes financial hardship. Every financial error can yield knowledge that improves future planning.

Another crucial habit is making regular adjustments to a budget. Living conditions, priorities, income, and obligations all fluctuate over time. A budget that was effective a few months ago might not be suitable now. While relocating to a new house may result in more expenses, a new job may result in higher income. Adjustments may also be necessary for education, family obligations, transportation needs, and shifting financial objectives. Periodically reviewing the budget guarantees its continued usefulness. The goal of updating it is to make the system more appropriate for the present situation rather than to give up on financial discipline.

In the end, effective budgeting practices result in more than just increased monthly spending control. They gain self-assurance, alertness, discipline, and patience. A young adult who consistently keeps an eye on their finances is better equipped to make more significant financial decisions in the future. Before income rises, the ability to effectively manage a modest income can offer invaluable expertise. The same practices can help keep lifestyle inflation from eating up every extra dollar as earnings rise. When income increases, a financially disciplined person might use some of the extra funds for savings, investments, debt reduction, and worthwhile objectives rather than immediately boosting spending.

The most crucial lesson is that consistent activity, as opposed to sporadic effort, is what makes budgeting successful. Stronger financial behavior is a result of planning purchases, monitoring finances on a regular basis, managing debt, reducing emotional spending, setting reasonable limits, automating saves, anticipating unforeseen expenses, and learning from failures. Even while these behaviors might seem insignificant on their own, they have a cumulative effect over months and years. A person who continuously develops better financial practices has more control over their finances and more ability to make decisions based on priorities rather than financial constraints. As a result, creating a budget becomes more than just a monthly task. It turns into a useful strategy for fostering self-control, safeguarding advancement, and strengthening the basis for future financial independence.

Creating Your Spending Roadmap

When a budget transforms a person's decision-making process rather than just being a set of figures, it becomes valuable. Making a spending plan is important since funds are scarce and demands, obligations, desires, and long-term objectives continue to vie for attention. Without a defined plan, it's simple to spend based on instinct, emotion, or convenience and later realize that crucial financial priorities have been overlooked. Every accessible sum of money has a purpose before it vanishes thanks to a sensible spending plan. When used regularly, it can lessen financial uncertainty, boost self-esteem, boost savings, avoid needless debt, and make future objectives seem more attainable. It doesn't need a lot of money. It necessitates a readiness to make thoughtful decisions regarding the available income.

The transition from reactive to purposeful spending is the biggest shift that happens when a spending roadmap is implemented. A person starts asking how available money should be spent before spending occurs rather than whether there is enough money left over after spending. This minor shift in perspective can have a significant impact in real life. A young adult who used to have little money left over at the end of each month might start saving as soon as they get paid. Future expenses can be taken into consideration before they become emergencies, necessary bills can be identified beforehand, and discretionary spending can be given a reasonable limit. The outcome is more than just an improved written plan or spreadsheet. More control over daily financial decisions is the outcome.

Ignoring a spending roadmap might lead to a tendency that gets harder to break. Small purchases can covertly deplete funds intended for more important purposes when spending is not monitored or planned. Regular meal orders, entertainment purchases, convenient transportation, or purchases made just because they are available are all possible. On its own, each expense might not seem like much. On the other hand, recurring costs might add up to a significant monthly sum. The person may rely on credit or borrow from others if there is no money left over for savings or unforeseen expenses. Financial strain may eventually result from this, which could have been avoided with earlier planning.

The emotional experience of handling money is likewise altered by a spending roadmap. Uncertainty about future commitments or the safety of current expenditure are common causes of financial uncertainty. Boundaries provided by a well-defined plan facilitate decision-making. There is less need to start from scratch when one is aware of how much money is available for savings, entertainment, transportation, food, and other priorities. Instead of being a punishment, the budget becomes a guide. Additionally, since money set aside for personal enjoyment can be spent without the same degree of guilt or uncertainty, it can make responsible spending more pleasurable.

Take a real-world example of a young adult who gets twenty thousand pesos a month. Without a plan, the person spends money on amusement, buys meals whenever it's convenient, pays bills when they come in, and occasionally makes purchases online. There is hardly any money left by the last week of the month. Before the next pay check comes in, the person makes a spending plan rather than just choosing to spend less. First, essential costs are determined. A set sum is put into savings. Food and transportation are subject to reasonable restrictions. A tiny sum is set aside for fun. The remaining funds are set aside for unforeseen expenses. Not all pleasurable expenses are eliminated by the individual. Spending instead becomes deliberate. After a few months, the individual has savings that they did not have before and a better idea of how much can be spent without risk.

This can have an impact on real life, as demonstrated by a short narrative. Daniel, a young man, thot that since he was making enough money to pay his bills, budgeting wasn't important. He was financially secure each payday and spent money freely in the first half of the month. However, he frequently started worrying about food and transportation expenses around the end of each month. When an unforeseen school-related obligation arose one month, Daniel's account was almost completely depleted, and he needed to borrow money. He made the decision to attempt a straightforward expenditure plan. Every payday, he set aside money for savings and necessities before thinking about leisure or optional items. For flexible expenses, he also established a weekly spending cap. Although the first month wasn't ideal, he discovered where his money was going. After a few months, regular spending no longer startled him. His earnings had not improved significantly. His financial habits had improved.

Considering a budget as a road map instead of a cage is a helpful metaphor. A road map does not stop a traveler from having fun. It merely displays the traveler's destination, the remaining distance, and the possible directions. A traveler may still go without a road map, but they run the risk of making needless detours or becoming lost. Money functions similarly. It is not necessary to restrict every peso in order to implement a spending roadmap. It gives guidance so that the destination is supported by spending. The path may alter as conditions do. Knowing your direction and making deliberate choices along the road are crucial.

By the end of this chapter, you will be able to identify spending patterns that hinder your ability to meet significant financial goals, make a realistic spending roadmap that links your income with necessary expenses, savings, personal priorities, and future goals, and modify your spending choices when your income, obligations, or priorities change. These results make sense because a budget shouldn't be made once and then forgotten. It ought to evolve into an adaptable decision-making framework that grows with your life.

You may implement this right away with the aid of a straightforward framework known as the Roadmap technique. Record is the first step. Put your regular spending and dependable sources of revenue in writing. Both obligatory and discretionary expenses should be included. Organize is the second stage. Divide expenditure into categories such as future objectives, personal spending, financial priorities, and necessities. Assigning is the third phase. Prior to spending available income, give it a purpose. Instead of waiting to see what's left, this involves allocating a certain amount to savings or other financial priorities. Measurement is the fourth step. Compare the monthly actual spending to the plan. Without passing judgment on yourself, look for distinctions. Adjust is the fifth stage. If an expense exceeded your budget, identify the reason for the discrepancy and make any necessary revisions to the plan. Repeat is the sixth step. Make a better plan for the following month by using the lessons learned from the previous one.

Because it views budgeting as a continuous process, the Record Organize Assign Measure Adjust Repeat approach is effective. Because they make unrealistic plans based on what they wish they would spend rather than what they actually spend, many people struggle with budgets. A realistic route map ought to be truthful. The plan should account for any costs associated with food, transportation, communication, family obligations, or personal necessities. Making impressive-looking numbers is not the aim. Developing a strategy that can withstand everyday living is the aim.

You can finish the first step today. Examine the funds you anticipate receiving in the upcoming month. Next, list all of your recognized responsibilities. Next, look at your previous expenditures and calculate how much you typically spend on flexible expenses. Next, choose how much should be set aside for savings or another crucial aspect of your finances. Determine what is left over for optional expenditure after these amounts are visible. This procedure can tell you right away if your existing way of living is compatible with your income. If it doesn't, you've found the issue early enough to fix it.

There should be space for reality in a budget plan. There will be unforeseen costs. Prices are subject to change. Income varies. Social interactions may take place. Family needs may come up. Thus, flexibility is necessary for a useful budget. The budget may be overly strict if every peso is allocated so strictly that one unforeseen expense ruins the entire plan. Creating a tiny, adaptable category can aid in absorbing common surprises. Emergency funds can eventually offer an extra degree of security.

Understanding the difference between fixed and variable expenses is another crucial application. In general, fixed costs are predictable and challenging to alter rapidly. Flexible spending is frequently easier to modify. This difference aids in determining the realistic areas where changes can take place. Reducing rent or tuition might not be the best course of action if they cannot be altered right away. When it comes to eating out, entertainment, subscriptions, shopping, and convenience purchases, a person might have greater control. Eliminating anything enjoyable is not the goal. Focusing efforts where change is feasible is the goal.

Making better decisions before big purchases is another benefit of using a spending plan. Before making a costly purchase, consider whether it will fit into your current budget; if it doesn't, decide if the item is significant enough to alter another priority. As a result, there is a beneficial delay between desire and action. In certain cases, the response is in the affirmative, and the purchase can be made sensibly. In other cases, waiting will avoid needless financial strain, and the response will be no. The fact that the choice is made consciously as opposed to instinctively is a significant improvement.

When budgeting is linked to certain objectives, it becomes particularly effective. Without a goal, saving might be challenging because the benefit is far off. The behavior has more significance when it is saved for an emergency fund, education, a car, a house, travel, career advancement, or future independence. Saying no to things that don't further that goal is made easier when one understands why money is being conserved. As a result, a spending roadmap becomes more than just a system of restrictions. It turns into a means of focusing current resources on potential futures.

Avoiding comparing your financial strategy to someone else's is also crucial. It is possible for two individuals to have entirely different spending, obligations, earnings, and objectives. Your situation should be reflected in a spending plan. What counts is whether your financial behavior is improving and whether your spending aligns with your own values. Increased knowledge, fewer wasteful spending, more savings, less financial stress, and improved readiness for future requirements are all indicators of progress.

Asking reflection questions can help you put this lesson into practice. Currently, where does the majority of your monthly income go? Which spending pattern diverts funds from things that are more important to you? Prior to the start of optional spending, which financial priority should receive funds? Which cost could you cut without materially lowering your standard of living? What adjustment can you make with your next pay check that will improve your financial situation right away?

Making a spending plan ultimately comes down to deciding what is important. Since money spent in one location cannot be spent in another at the same moment, every financial action involves a trade-off. That does not imply that spending has to become boring or constrained. It implies that expenditures should be in line with goals. Priorities become more apparent when funds are budgeted before being spent. Errors become valuable knowledge rather than sources of embarrassment when expenses are examined honestly. Consistent modifications strengthen the financial plan.

The most efficient spending plan is not the most intricate one. It is the one you can comprehend, adhere to, evaluate, and modify. A straightforward strategy that is continuously carried out is more beneficial than a complex plan that is dropped after a few weeks. Start with your knowledge. Keep a record of the events. Give your money a direction. Examine the outcomes. Make changes. The procedure should then be repeated. These routine activities have the potential to alter your perception of money over time significantly.

Rarely does one flawless choice lead to financial advancement. It develops as a result of numerous conscious little choices. These choices are given shape by a spending roadmap. It facilitates the transformation of income into deliberate action, spending into thoughtful decisions, and financial uncertainty into better planning. When the path of today's money is obvious, it becomes easier to approach the future. Start with your income, your obligations, and your most important objectives. Give each portion of your money a purpose, honestly assess your progress, and keep refining the path as your life evolves. Greater independence and confidence tomorrow can result from having a clear financial orientation today.

CHAPTER III

Developing Saving Habits

Savings Foundations

The first step in building a savings foundation is realizing that saving money is more than just setting aside what's left over after spending. It is a conscious financial practice that increases one's control over current decisions and prospects for the future. Early savings education can have long-term benefits for young adults. Saving lowers reliance on borrowing, builds the discipline required for long-term financial growth, protects against unforeseen costs, and generates resources for significant objectives. Even if the first savings may be modest, the habit itself can grow in value as income increases and financial obligations shift.

Knowing why saving is important is the first step in creating a solid foundation for saves. While money saved opens up opportunities for the future, money invested right away yields benefits in the here and now. Education, housing, business prospects, travel, family obligations, and other worthwhile objectives can all be financed with savings. When unforeseen costs arise, it can also offer comfort. Even a minor financial emergency might become stressful if there are no reserves since there might not be enough money to tackle it. A person who has savings is more flexible and does not have to rely on credit cards, loans, or other types of borrowing right away.

It takes more consistency than perfection to form the habit of saving. Many people think they must have a high income before they can start saving, yet waiting for the ideal financial circumstances might cause a significant habit to be postponed for years. Frequent small-scale savings can be more beneficial than sporadic large-scale savings. Developing consistency is the goal of starting small. Savings can progressively rise as income increases or wasteful spending is cut once it becomes a regular part of one's financial routine. Early adoption of this practice puts a young adult in a better position to profit from future income rises.

Treating savings as a regular financial obligation rather than a voluntary activity is one helpful strategy. Before discretionary spending starts, a predetermined portion of money might be allocated to savings. This strategy lessens the incentive to spend all available funds. Because the funds are transferred into a savings account automatically each time income is received, automatic transfers can further simplify the procedure. Instead of relying just on motivation, the idea is to make saving a standard aspect of money management.

Different goals for various kinds of savings should also be included in a savings foundation. Goal-based savings are meant for anticipated future needs, whereas emergency savings are meant to cover unforeseen costs. Organizing savings can be achieved by keeping these goals clear. While another savings account might be used for education, a significant purchase, travel, or future housing expenses, an emergency reserve might help cover an unforeseen repair or temporary loss of income. Setting distinct objectives can help track progress and lessen the temptation to utilize funds meant for one item to pay for something unrelated.

Because financial difficulties frequently occur without warning, emergency funds are particularly crucial. An unforeseen expense related to housing, transportation, technology, family obligations, or work may arise. If there isn't a reserve, the cost could need to be paid for using a loan or put on a credit card. Interest fees and further financial strain may result from this. An emergency fund serves as a safeguard. Although it can lessen the financial effect of unforeseen occurrences, it cannot stop them from occurring. Over time, increasing security can be achieved by progressively building this reserve.

Being conscious of one's spending habits is also necessary for saving. It could still be challenging to conserve money if income rises, but spending automatically increases at the same rate. When someone grows accustomed to more costly meals, entertainment, travel, clothes, subscriptions, or other lifestyle choices, this tendency may occur. Increasing the amount saved as income increases is one strategy to bolster savings. A portion of the gain might go toward future objectives rather than letting every extra peso or dollar vanish into new expenses. This strikes a balance between saving for future requirements and enjoying current income.

Separating short-term expenditures from long-term savings is another crucial idea. It is simpler to employ savings on a casual basis when they are combined with regular spending money. A psychological barrier that promotes more deliberate choices can be created by keeping savings in a different account. The account doesn't have to be difficult. It is important that the funds are explicitly designated for a certain purpose. Observing advancement toward a goal can also serve as a source of inspiration, as each contribution turns into tangible proof of progress.

Additionally, saving ought to be linked to particular objectives. A vague goal, like wanting to save more, might not be sufficient to inspire people to alter their spending patterns. Direction is created by a well-defined aim. A person may choose to amass funds for a future business opportunity, save for school, develop an emergency fund, or get ready for a significant purchase. It is simpler to determine whether a purchase is worth postponing the goal when the reason is obvious. A person can make decisions based on priorities rather than impulse by weighing short-term satisfaction against long-term value.

Someone shouldn't give up saving entirely due to financial difficulties. Some months may see a drop in income, an increase in expenses, or the need to use funds for an emergency. It is not a sign that the savings habit has failed when money is used for a true need. The emergency reserve did, in fact, accomplish its goal. Rebuilding what was used is a crucial next step. This kind of thinking keeps short-term setbacks from turning into long-term financial disappointment. Financial plans should be modified when conditions change because saving is an ongoing activity.

Future investments are also supported by a solid foundation of savings. While saving and investing have different goals, they can complement one another. While investments can be used for longer-term growth, savings offer easily accessible money for emergencies and immediate necessities. A person should set up a suitable savings account and be aware of the hazards before making an investment. If an emergency subsequently causes a person to sell investments at a bad time, there is no point in investing money for long-term growth. Prioritizing savings can provide the steadiness required for a more deliberate approach to investing.

Another crucial aspect of saving is its emotional component. While saving takes time, spending might yield instant gratification. Advertising and societal pressure that promotes continuous consumption are all around young adults. It can be challenging to match friends' ostentatious attire, gadgets, vacations, cars, or lives. Comparing one's attractiveness to one's own finances might lead to wasteful spending. A person with a strong savings mindset is able to understand that financial success is not determined by how much is on display. A developing emergency fund or a continuously rising savings balance are examples of quiet financial progress that may be significantly more valuable than outward expenditures.

Over time, saving becomes more than just a way to balance your finances. It builds confidence, self-control, patience, and planning skills. Every successful contribution strengthens the conviction that actions made today can help achieve future objectives. As savings increase, significant expenditures may require less borrowing, opportunities may become simpler to seize, and financial emergencies may become less terrifying. Because not every unforeseen circumstance calls for quick borrowing or sacrifice, someone with funds has more options.

In the end, deliberate choices made repeatedly over time build solid savings foundations. Understanding the purpose of saving, setting relevant goals, monitoring spending, consistently setting away money, creating emergency reserves, and safeguarding savings from wasteful spending are the first steps in the process. Even while the amount saved today might not seem like much, over time, regular contributions might produce significant resources. More significantly, the practice trains one to think about possibilities for the future rather than just their current desires. Income that would otherwise be squandered is transformed into a resource that can offer freedom, opportunity, and security through saving. Early establishment of this foundation gives young adults a strong financial habit that can help them make wise decisions and maintain stability over the course of their lives.

Emergency Savings

Since unforeseen costs can arise at any point in life, emergency funds are among the most crucial components of a solid financial foundation. Even if a person meticulously plans their monthly expenditures, they may still have to deal with unforeseen medical bills, auto repairs, broken household appliances, temporary job loss, urgent travel, or other costs that were not factored into their normal budget. An unforeseen circumstance might easily result in borrowing, missing payments, credit card charges, or financial stress if funds aren't placed aside for these circumstances. A person can react to challenging situations without totally upsetting their regular financial stability thanks to emergency savings. Early adoption of this behavior can boost a young adult's self-esteem and independence while decreasing their reliance on friends, family, loans, or costly credit when issues emerge.

Knowing why emergency funds should be maintained apart from regular expenditure is the first step toward creating emergency reserves. Goals like school, travel, a new computer, a car, a house, or future investments could be the focus of regular saves. The goal of emergency savings is different. They are intended for circumstances that are essential, unforeseen, and challenging to delay. Maintaining this difference makes it easier to avoid using emergency funds for regular expenses. The financial safety vanishes if funds set aside for emergencies are routinely squandered on leisure, dining, shopping, or planned expenditures. A distinct emergency fund might provide a practical and psychological barrier that makes it simpler to save the funds for circumstances that actually call for them.

Due to differences in living arrangements, monthly expenses, income stability, and financial responsibilities, each person will require a different amount of emergency reserves. A young adult who pays their own rent, utilities, transportation bills, and other home expenses may have different emergency needs than a young adult who lives with relatives. A person whose income fluctuates from month to month may be exposed to different hazards than someone whose income is steady. It is preferable to start with a realistic amount and progressively increase from there rather than being frustrated by a big savings goal. Establishing a little financial cushion to cover tiny unforeseen costs can be the first goal. The savings target might increase over time once that initial buffer is set.

It's more crucial to be consistent than to start with a lot. Because consistent contributions add up, a person who consistently saves a small amount can make significant progress. Because it regards emergency savings as a financial priority rather than an afterthought, saving right away after getting income can be particularly beneficial. There might not be much money left if one waits until all other costs have been covered. A stronger habit is formed by setting aside a certain amount in advance. As income and expenses fluctuate, the amount can be modified. The secret is to make frequent contributions, even if they seem insignificant.

A realistic grasp of monthly spending is also necessary for emergency savings. One should be aware of the approximate cost of necessities before determining the level of protection required. To ascertain how much money would be needed at a time of financial trouble, one can examine housing, food, utilities, transportation, communication, insurance, debt commitments, and other important expenses. This knowledge aids in transforming emergency savings from a theoretical concept into a realistic financial objective. Rather than merely stating that more money should be saved, one might ascertain, depending on real-world situations, what amount would offer significant protection.

Building up emergency funds is crucial since it protects against short-term income loss. Layoffs, fewer hours worked, business challenges, career changes, or personal situations can all create unforeseen changes in employment. The stability of an employer or the overall economy cannot be entirely controlled by an individual who performs well at work. Having cash on hand can give you time to look for another opportunity without having to worry about falling behind on important bills right away. While emergency funds can provide much-needed breathing room, they do not completely remove financial distress. Making deliberate choices rather than settling for the first alternative just because there isn't enough money left might be made easier when critical expenses can be covered for a while.

Long-term financial objectives can also be safeguarded by emergency savings. Consider a person who is investing for the future or saving for school when a significant repair is unexpectedly required. In the absence of an emergency fund, the individual could have to liquidate investments or take out long-term savings during a difficult moment. This may result in more expenses and a slowdown in financial growth. Money designated for other uses can be safeguarded with the help of a separate emergency reserve. In this sense, emergency reserves serve purposes beyond just covering unexpected expenses. They aid in maintaining an overall financial plan's framework.

Choosing a location for emergency savings is another crucial factor. When a real need arises, emergency funds must be available, but they shouldn't be so handy that it becomes tempting to spend carelessly. Accessibility and independence from regular expenses can be balanced with an appropriate savings account. Maximizing returns at the expense of availability is not the aim. The main purposes of emergency finances are access and security. Rather than generating the maximum return on investment, their primary value stems from their availability when needed.

When income is tight, it might be challenging to save for emergencies, but this does not imply the objective should be given up. One way to start is to look at spending trends and find places where tiny sums can be redirected. Additional ways to save money include cutting back on pointless subscriptions, minimizing impulsive purchases, cooking more often at home, avoiding convenience fees, or establishing spending caps. Progress can also be accelerated by additional revenue from freelance work, temporary employment, selling unwanted items, or other legal sources. The goal is to intentionally strike a balance between current expenditure and future security rather than to eliminate every pleasurable expense.

Setting guidelines for using emergency reserves is just as crucial. The account might eventually turn into a regular spending account in the absence of explicit guidelines. Setting aside funds for significant requirements that are unforeseen and challenging to meet with regular monthly cash flow is a helpful idea. Rebuilding the emergency reserve should become a top financial priority if it is used. For instance, once the immediate issue has been fixed, the person can temporarily raise savings contributions if an urgent repair necessitates a sizable withdrawal. The protection that was in place before the emergency is restored by rebuilding the fund.

There are psychological advantages to emergency savings as well. Anxiety can be brought on by financial uncertainty, particularly when someone is aware that a single unforeseen expense could ruin a whole month. You may feel more in control if you have money set up for emergencies. The individual is aware that not every unforeseen circumstance will turn into a financial emergency right away. Because financial decisions are less likely to be motivated by fear, this confidence can enhance decision-making. Instead of stressing about how to get money at the last minute, someone with an emergency cushion might be able to concentrate on finding a solution.

Additionally, the practice of emergency savings imparts important lessons about planning and postponing gratification. Young adults frequently struggle to balance living in the moment with planning for the future. Emergency reserves show that being frugal doesn't have to mean fully sacrificing enjoyment in the present. Rather, it necessitates acknowledging that future requirements also demand consideration. Even while putting money aside now might not pay off right away, it establishes protection that could grow to be quite useful in the future. An essential financial talent that can affect debt management, investing, saving, and other aspects of life is the capacity to postpone some expenses in order to increase security.

In the end, emergency funds are a sign of readiness rather than gloom. Putting money aside for emergencies does not imply that unpleasant things will happen. It entails accepting that life is unpredictable and making the decision to be ready for situations that aren't always under your control. A substantial emergency fund can lessen reliance on debt, safeguard significant financial objectives, offer flexibility when income fluctuates, and increase peace of mind. Early adoption of this practice can benefit young adults in ways that go well beyond a single unforeseen expense. Every donation increases financial stability and upholds the notion that funds should be used for both immediate needs and long-term security. The objective is to provide sufficient financial security to deal with unforeseen circumstances rather than to anticipate every potential issue. Emergency savings can develop into a reliable safety net that promotes increased independence and long-term financial security with perseverance, consistency, and frequent assessment.

Growing Savings

One of the most crucial habits a young adult can form is increasing their savings since it gives them flexibility, financial stability, and more influence over their future choices. Keeping cash in an account is not the only way to save money. It involves cultivating the self-control to postpone some expenditures today in order to free up funds for future opportunities and critical requirements. Early adoption of a regular savings habit helps protect against emergencies, be ready for big purchases, and progressively accumulate the funds required for long-term financial prosperity. The most crucial idea is to start with what is feasible and maintain consistency instead of waiting for the ideal financial circumstance.

The first step in increasing savings is realizing the importance of saving. Unexpected costs can quickly turn into financial emergencies if there are no savings. A person may be forced to borrow money when there is no reserve due to a broken appliance, an urgent need for transportation, a brief loss of income, school costs, a family obligation, or any other unforeseen circumstance.

Taking out a loan in an emergency might increase interest expenses and complicate recovery. A person can react to unforeseen circumstances without instantly relying on credit because of the financial cushion that savings offer. This lessens the anxiety brought on by uncertainty and fosters a sense of security.

When saving is linked to future objectives, it also offers flexibility. A young adult may wish to buy dependable transportation, pursue further education, relocate to a better house, launch a small business, travel, provide for family members, or get ready for future investments. These objectives frequently call for funds that are not readily available. Frequent saving breaks down big goals into smaller, easier-to-achieve steps. A person might break a significant financial goal into recurring payments rather than seeing it as something far off or unachievable. Every contribution shows advancement and strengthens the conviction that significant objectives may be accomplished with persistent work.

Knowing how much money is accessible is the first step in creating a realistic savings plan. Income should be weighed against debt repayment, other financial obligations, and necessary expenses. This allows one to calculate the amount that can be saved each pay period in a reasonable manner. It is not necessary to begin with a substantial sum. Because it creates the behavior, saving a tiny portion of income might be beneficial. The amount saved can progressively rise as income rises or expenses fall. Making an outstanding contribution once and then stopping is not as significant as consistency.

Treating savings as a regular financial commitment is one helpful strategy. Before making discretionary purchases, a person can choose to save a certain amount rather than saving whatever is left over after spending. By transferring funds into a savings account as soon as income is received, automatic transfers can facilitate this process. Repeatedly having to make the same choice is lessened by automation. Additionally, it establishes a division between funds available for daily expenses and funds meant for future uses. The procedure can eventually become nearly automatic, enhancing financial discipline without requiring continuous work.

Giving savings specific uses is also beneficial. It can be challenging to determine the intended use of funds if they are kept in a single, homogeneous sum. Emergency savings, short-term purchases, education, travel, significant life events, and future investments are examples of distinct objectives. By associating each contribution with a significant goal, naming a purpose can increase motivation. For instance, setting aside money on a regular basis for an educational objective could be more inspiring than merely attempting to boost one's financial account. Saving becomes a visible component of a bigger strategy when it has a purpose.

Since an emergency fund safeguards other financial objectives, it usually deserves extra consideration. If using money saved for a big purchase or trip will leave the person without any financial security, it might not be prudent to utilize it for an unforeseen expenditure. This issue can be avoided by creating a distinct emergency fund. Income, job security, necessities, and personal obligations all influence how much is needed. Someone raising a family may have different needs than a young adult with few financial responsibilities. Establishing a reserve and progressively strengthening it as conditions change is a crucial principle.

Reducing wasteful spending is also crucial to increase savings. This does not imply doing away with all pleasurable activities. Balance is essential for sustainable saving. A financial plan may become challenging to stick to if it is so restricted that a person is unable to enjoy anything. Rather, the objective is to identify low-value expenditures and reallocate a portion of those funds to worthwhile endeavors. Additional savings can be achieved without drastically altering one's lifestyle by cutting back on eating out, reviewing subscriptions, restricting impulsive purchases, comparing costs, or delaying the purchase of non-essential products. When small changes are made repeatedly, they might grow to be large.

Another crucial aspect of increasing funds is avoiding lifestyle inflation. It can be tempting to boost spending when income rises instantly. Increased income could result in more costly accommodation, transportation, entertainment, clothes, and other purchases. While some lifestyle changes may be justified, financial advancement may be impeded if every increase in income is converted into an increase in expenses. Dividing extra money between better living conditions and more stable finances is a preferable strategy. A person can profit from increased earnings and build future resources by increasing savings when income grows.

Additionally, savings should be shielded against needless temptation. It may be simpler to inadvertently spend savings if all available funds are kept in a daily spending account. Keeping savings and regular money apart can lead to psychological barriers. While decreasing the possibility that the funds will be utilized for regular purchases, a dedicated savings account can help track progress. Motivation can also be strengthened by routinely reviewing the account. Observing the balance increase offers concrete proof that sound financial practices are having an impact.

Savings growth may seem sluggish at first, but patience is crucial. Even if someone saves regularly for a few months, they might only make slight progress. This is not a sign of failure. Growth in finances frequently starts out slowly. Time and repetition are the sources of saving value. Contributions over several months or years can add up to a sizable sum. Additionally, the habit gets stronger with practice. When a young adult learns to save regularly now, they are building a skill that will be useful even when their income increases significantly in the future.

Eventually, savings may serve as the basis for investing and accumulating wealth. Some long-term savings may be allocated to suitable investments once emergency reserves are created and high-cost debt is under control. Other factors that come into play while investing include risk, diversification, time horizon, fees, and market changes. The key takeaway is that investment should enhance, not replace, financial stability. If funds are allocated to investments that are difficult to access, a person with substantial high-interest debt and no emergency savings may experience needless stress. Stability is typically the first step in a strong financial sequence, followed by more sophisticated growth tactics.

Increasing funds also improves judgment. There is less pressure to make bad financial decisions when one has money on hand. Instead of responding to a crisis right away, savings can give you time to think about your options. A person may be able to fix a car without taking out a costly loan if they have an emergency fund. When it comes to training, someone with education savings can have more options. A person may be more confident while investigating a professional possibility if their savings are increasing. Therefore, savings generate options rather than just balances.

Growing savings ultimately comes down to making it a habit to live wisely in the present while making plans for the future. Perfection, a large salary, or intricate financial plans are not necessary for this process. It calls for awareness, perseverance, consistency, and a readiness to put future needs ahead of current demands. Financial resilience is strengthened by every dollar saved. Every superfluous expense that is avoided results in more capacity. Every savings goal that is accomplished shows that focused effort may yield significant outcomes. Long-term objectives may become more achievable, opportunities may arise, and financial stress may diminish as savings accumulate. Therefore, one of the easiest and most effective strategies a young adult may use to create a stable and adaptable financial life is the habit of saving.

Strengthening Your Financial Cushion

When saving leads to more options, security, and self-assurance in daily life, it becomes genuinely worthwhile. Unexpected expenses are not uncommon, so having a financial cushion is important. Unexpected events may include a broken phone, an urgent need for transportation, a family obligation, a brief drop in income, educational costs, home repairs, or essential medical expenses. Even a modest expense can turn into a financial crisis if funds are not set aside for such circumstances. A person could have to borrow money, utilize a credit card, put off a crucial payment, or seek help from others. By adding a layer of safety between an unforeseen expense and a significant financial setback, building a financial cushion alters this situation. Money accumulation is not the only objective. In order to respond to life's obstacles without instantly sacrificing other objectives, the objective is to establish financial breathing room.

You can perceive unexpected occurrences differently if you put the concepts from this chapter into practice. You can start viewing every unexpected expense as a problem that can be solved rather than as a catastrophe. A financial safety net can give you time to consider your options. It can avoid having to borrow money at an inconvenient time. Maintaining regular financial obligations while addressing short-term challenges may also be made simpler. A small reserve can have a significant impact. However, even a person with little savings might not be able to handle every emergency; they are still in a better position than someone with nothing.

Financial vulnerability can spiral out of control if saving is neglected. There is no space for unforeseen needs when every pay check is spent right away. A person may seem to be financially secure during typical months, but as anything changes, they become heavily reliant on borrowing. Repetitive borrowing might result in higher interest rates and new commitments that deplete future earnings. Eventually, the first unforeseen expense is no longer the issue. The increasing financial strain brought on by not having a reserve becomes the issue. Thus, saving safeguards more than just cash. It prevents future earnings from being used to cover previous crises.

A financial safety net has psychological advantages as well. Living without reserves all the time might lead to anxiety because it makes every unforeseen circumstance seem dangerous. It can be reassuring to know that some money has been purposefully safeguarded. Financial worries do not go away as a result. Instead, the person is better able to react in a composed manner. A cushion can give you the assurance you need to deal with common unexpected expenses without having to make hasty financial decisions. Other decisions, such as long-term financial objectives, career choices, educational plans, and household choices, might also be influenced by this confidence.

Think about a real-world example. Consider a young worker who chooses to save aside a tiny sum from each pay check despite having a modest monthly income. The savings don't seem like much at first. But after a few months, the person has accumulated enough money for several weeks' worth of necessities. The person's main work tool breaks down one afternoon and needs an unforeseen repair. The person would most likely have to use costly credit or borrow money if they had no savings. The repair can be paid for without interfering with rent, food, transportation, or other necessary commitments because there is a reserve. The unforeseen expense was not eliminated by the savings. They altered the individual's capacity to react to it.

This idea is demonstrated in a short narrative. After receiving her salary, a young woman named Maria would typically spend nearly all of it before her next pay check. Because of her low income, she thot it was hard to save. Her transportation expenses unexpectedly went up one month, and she struggled to get to work regularly. She took out a loan from a friend, promising to pay it back when she got paid again. She reevaluated her financial practices as a result of the encounter. Even though it didn't seem like much, she started saving a set amount right away after each pay check. Her finances remained small after a few months, but she had yet another unforeseen transportation issue. She covered the cost herself this time. Maria came to the conclusion that her savings amount was not the most significant difference. It was the knowledge that she had established a resource she could rely on in times of uncertainty in her everyday life.

Comparing a financial cushion to a car's shock absorber is a helpful comparison. When driving on an uneven road, a car encounters bumps and abrupt shifts. Every bump produces a severe impact in the absence of a shock absorber. With one, the impact of the uneven surface is lessened, and the car may keep moving. Financial life is comparable. The roadblocks are unforeseen costs. Although they lessen the impact, savings do not eliminate such bumps. Your ability to withstand common financial shocks without losing direction increases with the size and strength of your financial cushion.

By the end of this chapter, you will be able to calculate a reasonable savings amount that fits your current income and obligations, develop a reliable strategy for creating a safety net even in situations where your available income is constrained, and use your savings wisely when unforeseen costs arise without unduly interfering with your larger financial priorities. These results transform saving from a nebulous goal into a workable strategy. The goal is not to save the ideal amount right away. The goal is to develop a consistent behavior that gets stronger as your financial situation improves.

You can start right away with a straightforward structure known as the Cushion Builder approach. Identify is the first step. Examine your necessary monthly expenditures and decide which ones must go on even in the event of an unforeseen issue. Start is the second step. Select a reasonable sum that can be saved on a regular basis without making it impossible for you to meet your fundamental needs. Protect is the third stage. To reduce the likelihood of it being lost due to impulsive purchases, keep the money meant for emergencies apart from regular expenses. Grow is the fourth step. Consider allocating a portion of the extra money to your financial cushion whenever your income rises, your costs fall, or you receive unanticipated funds. Rebuilding is the fifth step. As soon as the crisis has been resolved, start rebuilding the cushion if you must spend your money for an actual emergency.

A straightforward cycle that can be sustained throughout time is produced by the Identify Start Protect Grow Rebuild technique. The most crucial step is to begin with a reasonable amount. You might give up if you try to save so much that you can't keep up the habit. An ambitious sum saved just once may not be as beneficial as a lesser amount saved regularly. Establishing reliability is the first stage's goal. It may be simpler to increase the amount after the habit is established.

Additionally, your first objective should be related to your unique situation. Someone who is in charge of rent, transportation, home bills, or dependents may require a different reserve than someone with low living expenses and steady family support. There isn't a single quantity that works for everyone. Creating a reserve that accurately represents your true financial obligations is what counts. Start by determining which costs would be most challenging to pay for in the event that income abruptly halted or an unforeseen need arose.

Keeping regular expenditures and emergency savings apart might also have a significant impact. It can be easy to perceive savings as additional spending money if they stay in the same location as money used for everyday expenditures. Establishing a distinct savings account can serve as a psychological barrier. The money's purpose becomes more apparent. It serves as a reminder that its purpose is protection rather than consumption. Maintaining the saving habit may be made simpler by this straightforward division.

Automating saving wherever possible is another helpful habit. You are less likely to inadvertently spend money if it is transferred into savings soon after income is received. The number of decisions needed to sustain the habit can be decreased by automation. The strategy incorporates saving into your regular financial routine rather than asking you every pay check if you should save. When conditions change, the amount can be modified, but the fundamental behavior stays the same.

Learning to differentiate between everyday needs and emergencies is another necessary skill for saving. An emergency fund shouldn't be used to cover every unforeseen expense. A true emergency typically involves a critical demand that cannot be adequately met by the regular expenditure plan or postponed. Generally speaking, a planned purchase, entertainment cost, discounted item, or needless update shouldn't be considered an emergency just because it wasn't budgeted for. Maintaining the reserve's purpose helps guarantee that it will be accessible when something truly significant happens.

Using savings in an emergency shouldn't be seen as a sign of failure. An emergency fund is meant to be used when needed. You have achieved precisely what the savings were intended to do if you use a portion of the reserve for a justifiable unforeseen expense. Rebuilding it is the next duty. This viewpoint keeps individuals from feeling bad about utilizing money for what it was meant to be used for. Because it is accessible when life becomes uncertain, a financial cushion is helpful.

Your financial cushion can increase in tandem with your salary. A higher lifestyle does not always follow from a pay raise. Before new spending patterns become ingrained, a portion of the extra money can bolster savings. Bonuses, presents, side income, and money received from finished work are all subject to the same rule. It is possible to accelerate growth without making significant compromises in daily living by allocating a percentage of unexpected or increasing income into financial reserves.

A crucial lesson about financial independence is also imparted by building a cushion. Being independent does not imply never requiring assistance. It entails improving your capacity to manage routine tasks using your own resources. That capacity grows with every dollar saved. The direction is important, but the process can be slow, particularly when money is tight. A person's foundation for future decisions is strengthened when they regularly accumulate financial reserves.

This lesson can be put into practice with the use of reflection questions. How much cash would you need to cover one reasonable unforeseen expense without taking out a loan? Which expense, if it happened this month, would be the most problematic? How much of your next salary might you actually save without compromising necessities? What spending patterns might you alter to allow for consistent saving? If you have to use your financial cushion and then rebuild it, how will you react?

There is more to saving than just seeing your account balance rise. The purpose is to generate choices. You may make decisions without instantly relying on debt thanks to savings, which can also give you time and flexibility. When circumstances change, having a financial buffer can help safeguard your progress and speed up your recovery from unforeseen events. Even though it starts out tiny, it's worth increases with consistency.

The most crucial step is to start now rather than waiting for the ideal financial circumstances. There might never be a month when saving is totally effortless. There will be ongoing obligations, shifting expenditures, and unforeseen charges. Therefore, saving must become a conscious priority rather than something that merely occurs when funds are available. A little bit of protection now can result in more protection later.

Start with what you can actually handle. Determine your basic necessities, set aside a consistent amount for savings, safeguard the funds from wasteful spending, and periodically assess your progress. Increase your funds when your situation improves. Use the reserve guilt-free when an emergency arises, then rebuild it. Your financial resilience is strengthened with each cycle.

Quietly, a substantial financial safety net is being constructed. Even though it might not be exciting right away, it's worth becomes clear when life gets uncertain. You may avoid tomorrow's issue from turning into tomorrow's debt with the money you safeguard today. Small sacrifices are converted into more stability through consistent saving, and more stability opens the door to wiser decisions. Start with a reasonable quantity, safeguard it purposefully, and continue expanding. One of the most useful safeguards you can provide for your future self is your financial cushion.

CHAPTER IV

Controlling Personal Debt

Understanding Debt

Since debt may affect almost every aspect of a young adult's financial life, understanding debt is one of the most crucial steps toward becoming financially responsible. Debt is neither inherently good nor bad. It is a financial commitment that lets someone spend money now with the promise to pay it back later, typically with extra expenses like interest and fees. The true question is whether the debt is manageable, affordable, and beneficial. Young adults can make decisions based on facts rather than feelings, pressure, or fleeting impulses when they understand how debt operates. Without this knowledge, borrowing can quickly develop into a habit that limits financial independence and restricts the flexibility of future income. Instead, when debt fits into a realistic financial plan and has a purpose, it may be used carefully with the right information.

Understanding the distinctions between the various types of debt is crucial. Repayment obligations are created by credit card balances, personal loans, student loans, auto finance, mortgage loans, and some installment purchases. A person may be able to acquire housing, transportation, education, or other assets that support long-term objectives with the aid of certain types of borrowing. Other types may result from frivolous purchases, impulsive spending, entertainment, or lifestyle decisions that offer momentary gratification without producing long-term value. Therefore, the reason for borrowing should be taken into account before the amount. A person is already cultivating a better relationship with debt if they ask why the money is required, whether the purchase is necessary, and whether repayment would conflict with significant financial objectives.

Another crucial component of comprehending debt is interest. When a borrower takes out a loan, the lender often charges interest in exchange for granting access to the money. The amount of additional money the borrower may eventually have to pay depends on the interest rate. Even when the initial amount borrowed is affordable, a high interest rate debt can become costly. Because interest can build up over time, credit card debt can be very expensive when balances are not paid. Making just the minimum payment might keep an account current, but it can also increase the total cost and lengthen the repayment duration. Instead of concentrating simply on the initial amount they receive, borrowers can see the full cost of borrowing by understanding the relationship between the original balance, interest rate, payment amount, and repayment time.

Monthly cash flow is also impacted by debt. Each mandatory payment signifies funds that must be allocated to a previous choice rather than being available for present requirements or future objectives. With many loan installments, a young adult may have less money for emergencies, education, vacation, investing, saving, or other goals. This does not imply that borrowing should be avoided at all times. It implies that the total financial picture must account for debt payments. A person should think about their present income, necessary spending, savings, current obligations, and future financial responsibilities before taking out a loan or using credit. When combined with rent, food, transportation, utilities, insurance, savings, and other obligations, a payment that seems reasonable on its own may become challenging.

Making the distinction between needs and wants is one of the best habits for managing debt. People may borrow money for things they can't afford due to emotional spending. Unnecessary borrowing can be encouraged by advertising, societal pressure, convenience, and the need to sustain a specific lifestyle. Debt can eventually become a regular aspect of expenditures once a person feels at ease using credit for necessities. This may lead to a vicious cycle whereby new loans are taken out to pay for regular bills or past debts. Gaining the ability to think things through before borrowing gives you the chance to assess whether the purchase is really necessary. A short-term desire can be kept from turning into a long-term financial burden by delaying a purchase, accumulating money in advance, or selecting a less expensive option.

Because credit cards can make spending seem easier and less urgent, they merit particular consideration. Because borrowed money does not instantly leave a bank account, it may lessen the emotional impact of a purchase. The financial obligation still exists, though. Understanding the interest rate, fees, due date, credit limit, and repayment conditions is essential for responsible credit utilization. Keeping borrowing under control and avoiding needless interest charges can be achieved by paying the entire debt on time whenever feasible. Long-term balance carrying can greatly increase the cost of routine purchases. Rather than viewing available credit as more money, a prudent borrower views it as a financial instrument.

Knowing one's credit history is also necessary to comprehend debt. When determining whether to approve future borrowing and what terms to offer, lenders may review an individual's credit history. Creditworthiness can be influenced by a number of criteria, including length of credit history, outstanding debt, and payment history. Financial problems that may extend beyond the initial debt can result from failing to make payments or letting accounts get significantly past due. A better financial record can be established through prudent borrowing and on-time payments. Building credit, however, should never be used as a justification for needless borrowing. Credit management is not meant to boost spending power, but rather to show financial responsibility.

The idea that debt should be considered in light of future objectives is another crucial lesson. Building an emergency savings account, buying a house, launching a business, investing for retirement, or providing for a family are all possible goals for a young adult. Due to the commitment of income to repayment, excessive debt can cause these goals to be delayed. It is helpful to consider if the debt will help or hinder critical goals before taking out a loan. Borrowing for an expensive lifestyle purchase may serve a different financial purpose than borrowing for schooling that increases future earning potential. Even in cases where debt is beneficial, the borrower must decide if the anticipated advantages outweigh the expense and whether repayment is still feasible in other situations.

Consider a young worker who wants to buy a car and has a reliable source of income to gain a realistic understanding of debt. The employee takes into account the down payment, interest rate, loan period, insurance, fuel, maintenance, registration, and other transportation expenses in addition to the monthly loan payment. The employee also looks at current spending and savings objectives. This more comprehensive analysis might show that transportation could be provided by a less costly car without unduly straining the monthly budget. Therefore, the choice is based on whether the borrower can comfortably bear the full financial burden rather than just whether a lender will grant the loan.

Honesty is also necessary for managing debt. Financial issues are typically made worse by ignoring statements, avoiding account balances, or holding out hope that they would go away. If someone already has debt, they should be aware of the precise amount owed, the applicable interest rates, the due dates, and the percentage that each payment lowers the principal. A repayment plan can be created after the whole situation is known. Financial strain can be gradually reduced by prioritizing expensive debt, avoiding needless new borrowing, paying more than the statutory minimum when financially feasible, and allocating extra income toward repayment. Consistency is crucial. Rather than making a single, drastic financial decision, debt reduction is typically accomplished through a series of smart decisions.

In the end, comprehending debt is comprehending the connection between current decisions and future liberty. People can bring future revenue into the present by borrowing, but doing so requires a commitment. Future decision-making freedom decreases with the amount of income pledged to creditors. Financial habits that help shield young individuals from preventable hardship include prudent borrowing, cost comparison, reading contracts, differentiating necessities from wants, and regular payments. Additionally, they become more adept at using credit wisely when borrowing is actually required.

Respecting debt rather than being afraid of it is the aim. It is important to address debt with awareness, self-control, and a distinct goal. Cost, affordability, utility, and long-term effects should all be considered while making any borrowing decisions. When debt is handled properly, it can continue to be a controllable financial obligation rather than a continual source of anxiety. It can deplete funds, limit options, harm credit, and postpone crucial objectives when it is disregarded or misused. Early debt education enables young folks to make more deliberate financial decisions and create a future where their finances support their objectives rather than being dictated by previous purchases.

Managing Debt

Since borrowing can affect a person's decisions, cash flow, prospects, and long-term financial stability, managing debt is a crucial financial skill. By promising to pay back the cost over time, debt enables someone to get something today. When used wisely, borrowing can assist with funding housing, transit, education, and other necessities. However, if debt is used carelessly, it can become a burden that reduces future earnings. Understanding how debt functions is particularly important for young adults because early financial mistakes can have long-term effects. Understanding when debt is beneficial, how much can be managed, and how to keep borrowed funds from influencing future financial decisions are the objectives rather than necessarily avoiding all forms of borrowing.

Knowing exactly what is owed is the first step in controlling debt. Every loan should have its balance, interest rate, minimum payment, repayment schedule, fees, and due date understood. When the entire obligation is unknown, it is challenging to develop a repayment plan. A comprehensive picture of the financial condition can be obtained by recording or examining every account. This could show that while some obligations have high interest rates, others have very cheap prices. Knowing these distinctions makes it easier to decide which responsibilities require more focus. Debt does not go away if it is ignored. Honestly facing the numbers establishes the foundation for progress.

One of the most crucial ideas to comprehend while handling debt is interest. The amount borrowed does not always equal the amount that will be paid back in the end. Interest can greatly raise the overall cost, especially if amounts are not paid over extended periods of time. Even with regular payments, high interest debt can build rapidly and become challenging to repay. Because of this, concentrating just on the monthly payment may be deceptive. Even when a payment seems reasonable, the overall cost of payback is still rather substantial. A person can make better borrowing and repayment decisions if they comprehend the connection between interest, balance, and repayment time.

Another essential component of responsible debt management is timely payment. In addition to incurring additional costs, late payments may harm one's credit history. More significantly, persistent late payments might start a vicious cycle that makes it harder to manage financial issues. Missed deadlines can be avoided by setting up reminders, scheduling payment dates, or, when necessary, utilizing automatic payments. However, only when the user consistently has sufficient funds in the account should automated payments be utilized. Because good debt management requires both having a repayment plan and continuously adhering to it, organization is crucial.

A repayment plan needs to take the individual's financial circumstances into account. Because this strategy can lower the total amount of interest paid over time, some people find it advantageous to pay off the debt with the highest interest rate first. Others would want to start by eliminating a smaller balance because it gives them reason to win early. When used regularly, any strategy can be beneficial. Having a well-defined plan is more important than making sporadic additional payments. While extra funds are allocated to the selected priority, required minimum payments on other accounts should continue. When one debt is paid off, the money that was previously utilized for that payment can be applied to the subsequent obligation.

Controlling new borrowing is another aspect of managing debt. A frustrating cycle can result from paying off debt while continuously accruing new balances. A person should think about whether the purchase is essential, whether it can be postponed, whether saving for it is feasible, and whether the future payment would conflict with other goals before taking out a loan. Borrowing ought to be viewed as a commitment against future earnings. A portion of tomorrow's profits will already have a purpose if money is borrowed today. It is possible to avoid needless commitments by being aware of this trade-off.

Because credit cards can make spending seem easier than it actually is, they need special consideration. When used properly, a credit card can be an easy way to make payments, but it should never be viewed as extra money. Interest fees can eat up funds that could be used for savings or other objectives if someone consistently carries sums that cannot be paid back. Spending only what can be reasonably reimbursed and being aware of the account's terms are sound practices. While irresponsible credit use might result in long-term financial strain, responsible credit use can promote financial flexibility.

Including repayment as a budgeted item in a monthly budget makes managing debt easier. When money is left over at the end of the month, debt should not be viewed as something that needs to be paid. Housing, food, transportation, savings, and other significant costs should be included in the required payments. This makes it easier to see how much money has already been committed. The person may need to boost income, cut back on discretionary spending, or create a longer-term repayment plan if debt payments take up a significant portion of their income. Adjustments may be simpler if this issue is identified early.

Managing debt while increasing savings can also be crucial. While allocating all available funds to debt could seem sense, not having any emergency savings can put you at risk. The person might have to take out another loan if an unforeseen expense arises, which would reverse some of the payback progress. This issue can be avoided by keeping a small emergency fund. The right ratio of debt repayment to savings relies on personal circumstances, income stability, and interest rates. The overarching objective is to establish a financial system that both lowers debt and keeps new financial crises from necessitating further borrowing.

Understanding the emotional aspect of borrowing is a crucial component of debt management. Debt might lead to avoidance, irritation, fear, or embarrassment. People may ignore statements, put off payments, or refuse to check balances as a result of these feelings. Avoidance typically exacerbates the problem. Treating debt as a financial issue that can be examined and resolved gradually is a better strategy. A person's worth or aptitude is not determined by the amount due. Taking accountability and developing a workable improvement plan are what count. Even if progress could be sluggish, persistent action can make a difference.

Future prospects may also be impacted by debt. It may be more difficult to save, invest, relocate, pursue education, launch a business, or react to job changes if you have a lot of monthly obligations. Therefore, lowering debt might result in more than just a smaller sum. It may generate extra cash flow each month. After a debt is paid off, the funds that were previously utilized for payments can be put toward investments, savings, education, or other objectives. For this reason, debt reduction can play a significant role in long-term financial advancement.

Before signing contracts, careful thot must also be given to responsible debt management. Interest charges, fines, fees, variable rates, and other easily missed conditions may be included in loan contracts and credit agreements. Before accepting a loan, one should be aware of the entire financial responsibility. Asking questions or looking for trustworthy advice can help avoid expensive misunderstandings if the terminology is confusing. It's crucial never to assume that a loan is affordable just because the monthly payment seems reasonable. Always take the long-term impact and whole cost into account.

In the end, debt management is about managing future financial obligations instead of letting them dictate current decisions. Sometimes borrowing is beneficial, but it must be done with knowledge and self-control. A stronger financial position can be achieved by being aware of what is owed, comprehending interest, making timely payments, lowering high-cost balances, avoiding needless borrowing, keeping emergency funds, and routinely assessing progress. Debt doesn't have to be an ongoing burden. Balances can progressively decrease, and financial flexibility can rise with a well-defined plan and consistent behavior. As a result, you not only have less debt but also have more flexibility to allocate future earnings to worthwhile endeavors. Early debt management training can help young adults avoid many avoidable financial issues and build a stronger basis for long-term financial success, independence, and stability.

Avoiding Debt Problems

Since debt may affect almost every aspect of a person's financial life, avoiding debt issues is one of the most crucial financial skills a young adult can acquire. While borrowing money is not necessarily bad, taking on debt without knowing its cost, purpose, and payback obligations can lead to problems that get harder over time. When handled properly, credit cards, personal loans, payment plans, student loans, auto financing, and other borrowing options can offer helpful financial support. But when spending regularly surpasses income, payments are neglected, balances keep rising, or borrowing becomes a routine way to cover daily costs, debt becomes an issue. Early awareness of these risks enables young adults to make wise financial choices and steer clear of habits that may restrict their future freedom and prospects.

Knowing the difference between a required financial need and needless borrowing is one of the first steps to avoiding debt issues. A significant long-term objective, like education, dependable transportation, or a well-thought-out business investment, may be supported by some debt. Because every loan generates a future responsibility, borrowing should be done carefully even under these circumstances. Eventually, the funds acquired today must be reimbursed, typically with additional expenses. A person should consider whether the purchase is required, whether it can be postponed, whether savings could cover it, and whether the anticipated benefit outweighs the entire repayment amount before taking out a loan. Instead of making decisions solely on the basis of instant desire, this straightforward procedure promotes responsible thinking.

Another effective strategy to keep debt from becoming an issue is to live within your means. People frequently rely on credit to make up the difference when they consistently spend more than they make. The sums can seem reasonable at first, but frequent borrowing can start a vicious cycle where one payment triggers another loan or credit card debt. By outlining precisely how much money is available for housing, food, transportation, communication, entertainment, savings, and other needs, a realistic spending plan helps avoid this circumstance. It is simpler to find wasteful spending and make changes before borrowing is required when expenses and income are fairly matched.

Because credit cards can make spending seem less immediate, they call for special discipline. Because the purchase does not instantly lower the bank balance, paying with borrowed money may provide the impression that something is inexpensive. In actuality, the obligation persists and could get more costly if the debt is carried over from one month to the next. By using a credit card as a means of payment rather than as a source of additional cash, young adults can lower this risk. Ideally, purchases should only be made when sufficient funds are available to cover the remaining amount. Small amounts can be kept from becoming costly long-term liabilities by being aware of interest rates, minimum payments, fees, due dates, and credit restrictions.

Avoiding borrowing for lifestyle needs that exceed current income is another crucial rule. When expensive apparel, frequent dining out, entertainment, gadget upgrades, travel, and other discretionary items are frequently funded by credit, they can turn into sources of debt. Enjoying these things when they are reasonably priced is OK, but borrowing money to support a lifestyle can put a strain on finances. Saving for desired goods and allowing spending to occur once the required funds have been set aside is a better strategy. This lessens reliance on borrowed money while strengthening the link between earning, saving, and spending.

Additionally, emergency funds are crucial for avoiding debt issues. Unexpected costs are a part of everyday life. When there isn't enough money to cover an unforeseen expense, such as a car repair, a broken appliance, an urgent trip, or a brief lack of income, stress might result. Without funds, a person can quickly resort to expensive loans or credit cards. Because it establishes a financial cushion between an unforeseen circumstance and new debt, even a small emergency fund can offer significant protection. It is frequently more practical to build this reserve gradually rather than waiting until there is sufficient capital to establish a sizable fund right away.

Additionally, rather than concentrating solely on the monthly payment, young adults should carefully consider the entire cost of borrowing. A lengthier payback period can greatly raise the total amount paid, even if a loan may seem manageable due to its tiny monthly payment. Borrowing can be far more expensive than the initial purchase due to interest, administrative fees, late fees, and other expenses. Unpleasant surprises can be avoided by comparing several loan options and fully comprehending the repayment schedule before signing an agreement. A responsible borrower takes into account whether the payment will be reasonable in the event that income declines or other expenses rise, in addition to whether it fits within the current budget.

Being conscious of emotional spending is also necessary to avoid debt issues. Financial decisions can be influenced by stress, loneliness, social pressure, boredom, and the desire to seem successful. Unrealistic expectations about what people should own or experience can be created by advertising and social media. Debt can increase without the individual fully realizing it when spending turns into a means of controlling feelings or winning approval. Making more deliberate financial decisions can be achieved by learning better coping mechanisms for emotional stress. Waiting before making a significant purchase, talking to a trusted person about the choice, or putting the purchase's justification in writing can provide ample time to assess if the cost is indeed essential.

Regularly keeping an eye on debt instead of disregarding it is another beneficial habit. Sometimes people are afraid of what they could find, so they don't check loan details, credit statements, or account balances. Regretfully, avoiding financial information does not solve the issue. An accurate picture of financial commitments can be obtained by routinely checking balances, interest rates, due dates, and available credit. There are typically more possibilities for solving an issue if it is identified early. Missed payments, accruing interest, penalties, and a tarnished credit history can make recovery far more difficult if neglected for an extended length of time.

Making timely payments is another aspect of responsible debt management. A person's credit history may suffer as a result of late payments, which may also incur additional costs. The danger of inadvertently missing payments can be decreased by setting reminders, utilizing automatic payments where necessary, and maintaining a calendar of financial due dates. Automation shouldn't take the place of mindfulness, though. It is still necessary to keep enough money in the account to cover planned payments, and one should routinely check statements for errors or unanticipated costs.

Identifying warning indicators of high debt is equally crucial. Making only minimum payments, avoiding statements, repeatedly exceeding credit limits, using one credit card to pay another bill on a regular basis, relying on loans for needs, or feeling overburdened by monthly commitments are all signs that debt is getting harder to manage. Instead of being grounds to feel humiliated, these indicators could be used as motivation to take action. A short-term issue can be kept from developing into a long-term financial crisis by reviewing spending, cutting back on wasteful spending, raising income if feasible, and getting reliable financial advice.

The more profound lesson is that avoiding debt issues involves more than just declining to take out loans. It involves learning to make financial decisions based on affordability, purpose, timing, and potential outcomes. A person who is aware of these guidelines can use credit wisely without letting it dictate crucial choices. When revenue is not continuously used to cover previous purchases, financial independence becomes easier to achieve. Then, more funds can be allocated to investments, savings, education, personal objectives, and possibilities that increase future stability.

Early adoption of ethical borrowing practices can have long-term advantages. People are more flexible when it comes to changing professions, relocating, starting a business, pursuing further education, or reacting to unforeseen events when their debt is kept under control. They are able to make decisions based less on financial pressure and more on opportunity. Uncontrolled debt, on the other hand, can make people postpone crucial objectives because a large portion of their income is already devoted to repayment. Thus, avoiding needless debt safeguards more than just a bank account. It safeguards time, options, self-assurance, and the capacity to mold the future more freely.

In the end, debt should not be viewed as extra money but rather as a significant financial obligation. Before taking out a loan, a young adult should know why the money is needed, how much will be paid back, how long it will take, and how the commitment will impact future financial objectives. A solid defense against needless borrowing can be established by developing savings, managing expenditure, comprehending credit, making timely bill payments, and identifying emotional triggers. The objective is to comprehend debt sufficiently to use it responsibly rather than to be afraid of it. Money becomes a tool for advancement rather than a cause of ongoing financial strain when borrowing is handled with self-control and long-term understanding.

Moving Toward Financial Freedom

Personal debt management is important since the impact of debt extends beyond the amount due. It can affect the amount of money left over for investments, savings, emergencies, education, housing, family obligations, and personal objectives. Uncontrolled debt might progressively diminish financial freedom, although it can occasionally open doors to beneficial opportunities. A young adult may believe that every pay check already belongs to someone else if debt obligations take up a significant portion of their income. By raising the amount of money available for future objectives, lowering needless interest expenses, and fostering a clear awareness of commitments, responsible debt management can improve this scenario. Neglecting debt might have the opposite impact. Interest can increase small amounts, late payments can result in extra expenses, and recurrent borrowing can start a vicious cycle where new debt is taken on to cover previous commitments.

When financial actions are examined over time, the practical implications of debt management become evident. Because the immediate payment is small, a purchase made using borrowed funds may appear inexpensive. However, when interest and fees are taken into account, the whole cost may increase significantly. Money must continue to be used for a commitment long after the initial purchase has been forgotten, which may also reduce a person's flexibility in the future. Many financial errors can be avoided by learning to assess debt according to its entire cost rather than just its monthly payment. Avoiding all borrowing is not a prerequisite for responsible debt management. It entails knowing how much borrowing will cost, determining whether the benefit outweighs the expense, and making sure that repayment fits comfortably within the budget.

A young adult can gradually experience an increase in financial freedom once debt is under control. An obligation is lessened with each payment. More money becomes accessible for various uses when balances drop. Eventually, the funds that were previously used for debt might be used for investments, savings, education, business ventures, or important personal objectives. As a result, there is a significant financial shift. A person starts to use present revenue to create future chances rather than perpetually paying for past decisions.

Ignoring debt can make it harder to escape financial strain. Opening remarks may be avoided by someone who feels overwhelmed by the balance. Without knowing how long payback would take, they might merely make the minimum payments. While trying to lower current balances, they might keep utilizing credit. Additionally, they could borrow money from one source to pay back another. While the underlying issue persists, these actions may give the impression of progress. Debt cannot be eradicated by avoidance. It frequently makes the issue more costly.

By the end of this chapter, you will be able to determine which debts are the biggest burden on your present finances, develop a practical repayment plan that allocates funds to lowering debt while safeguarding necessities, and alter borrowing and spending habits that may result in future debt. These results make managing debt an active effort instead of a cause for concern.

Understanding your debts, making thoughtful payments, and forming routines that progressively improve your financial independence are the objectives.

A young adult with three debts provides a real-world illustration. One is a smaller balance with lesser expenses, another has a moderate interest rate, and a third has a comparatively high interest rate. Rather than making sporadic payments whenever funds are available, the individual computes the necessary payments, determines which debt is the most costly, and allocates extra funds to that amount while continuing to make the necessary payments on the remaining debts. The money that was previously utilized to pay off the first debt is transferred to the subsequent commitment. As a result, momentum increases. Even though the person isn't necessarily making more money, the money they do make is more productive because fewer resources are being used to pay off debt.

This shift is demonstrated in a short narrative. Carlo, a young employee, had accrued a number of minor debts from dining out, internet shopping, and needless borrowing. He kept making the minimal payments because none of the sums appeared to be significant on their own. He eventually came to the realization that a large portion of his monthly income was being used to pay off debts that had little long-term worth. Carlo made a list of all the balances, interest charges, necessary payments, and due dates rather than giving up. He made a repayment plan and ceased taking on new, pointless debt. Progress seemed sluggish at first. However, one balance vanished after a few months. The second debt started to decline more quickly after he rerouted that payment toward another obligation. When Carlo eventually paid off all of his debt, he realized that achieving a zero amount was not his greatest accomplishment. He had mastered the art of controlling the choices that first led to the debt.

Considering debt as a bag full of financial weight is a helpful image. It might not seem hard to carry one tiny item, but carrying a lot of extra stuff can make every step more challenging. The burden that must be carried into the future is represented by debt payments. Eliminating debt is similar to removing bulky items one at a time from a rucksack. As the weight drops, the trek gets simpler. The intention is to avoid feeling guilty about carrying the bag. Examining what is inside, getting rid of anything superfluous, and avoiding adding more weight without a good cause are the objectives.

The Debt Freedom Path is a straightforward framework that might offer a quick way to take action. Reveal is the first step. Put all of your debts in writing, along with the amount owed, interest rate, minimum payment, and due date. Setting priorities is the second phase. Determine which debt, based on cost, balance, or another intentional payback plan, needs more attention. Protect is the third stage. To prevent debt payback from causing another financial catastrophe, keep making the necessary payments and set aside enough cash for necessities. Attack is the fourth step. Avoid needless additional borrowing by allocating available excess funds to the chosen priority debt. Redirect is the fifth stage. Transfer the money that has been released from one loan to the subsequent one. Prevent is the sixth step. Determine the behavior that led to needless borrowing and create a rule that makes it less likely to happen again.

Because ambiguity frequently makes debt appear bigger and more terrifying than it actually is, the Reveal stage is particularly crucial. Clarity is produced when the entire image is written down. You can see precisely what is needed, as opposed to thinking hazily about owing money. This enables the creation of a practical plan and the calculation of priorities. While avoiding financial information could offer some emotional solace, confronting it offers the chance to take charge.

Selecting a plan that works for you is part of the Prioritize step. Because it can lower overall interest expenses, some people would rather concentrate on the debt with the highest interest rate. Others would favor paying off a lesser balance initially because it might be motivating to see a debt vanish. When used regularly, any strategy can be beneficial. The key idea is to choose a method carefully instead of making payments at random.

The Protect stage keeps debt repayment from becoming impractical. When an emergency arises, someone who devotes all of their available pesos to debt and has no money left over for necessities could have to take out another loan. Therefore, debt repayment should be balanced with necessary spending and appropriate financial security. Sometimes a tiny emergency fund might keep a small issue from turning into a debt.

Consistency is necessary for the Attack step. Even though extra payments might not seem like much, they can speed up development if they are made frequently. A portion of any extra money you make, cut back on wasteful spending, or discover a short-term means to raise cash on hand can be applied to the priority debt. Instead of waiting for one big sum of money to address everything, the goal is to build momentum.

Debt repayment can become more potent during the Redirect step. Let's say you have been making regular payments on one loan and eventually pay it off. Use the same amount toward the next loan rather than utilizing it on lifestyle purchases. Your ability to make repayments has essentially improved without necessitating a pay increase. This is among the best methods for building momentum.

The Prevent phase makes sure that eliminating debt doesn't just result in a new borrowing cycle. Find out what caused the debt in the first place. Was it an emergency, a lack of resources, social pressure, emotional spending, convenience purchases, inadequate income, or poor planning? Diverse reasons call for diverse remedies. Building savings could be the solution if the debt were caused by crises. Establishing a waiting period before purchases could be beneficial if impulsive purchases caused it. If income was inadequate, it might be essential to acquire useful skills or discover other sources of revenue.

Understanding the distinction between affordable and just payable is also necessary for managing debt. Even if a payment fits within one month's budget, it may be a bad financial choice over a number of years. Think about the period, interest rate, total repayment amount, and impact on future income before taking out a loan. Inquire as to whether the purchase is truly necessary, whether there is a less costly option, and whether it would be preferable to wait to save. These inquiries cause a halt between obligation and desire.

Additionally, credit should not be viewed as additional revenue but rather as a financial obligation. Eventually, borrowed funds must be paid back, frequently with extra expenses. A young adult finds it easier to spend more than they can afford when they start considering credit as a source of future income. Considering borrowing as a pledge against future resources is a better strategy. Future financial freedom is diminished to some extent by each additional debt.

Repaying debt can also present a chance to improve other financial practices. Continue saving and planning as balances deteriorate instead of letting every advancement turn into more lifestyle expenditures. The financial benefit may vanish if debt payments decline, but consumption rises right away. Redirecting liberated revenue toward more solid financial foundations is the aim.

It's also critical to understand that a person's destiny is not determined by their financial blunders. Due to bad choices, a lack of financial literacy, family situations, schooling, emergencies, or other factors, a young adult may already be in debt. Seldom does shame result in a practical financial strategy. Accountability does. The best course of action is to recognize the problem, comprehend its root causes, and implement workable solutions.

These concepts can be put into practice with the use of reflection questions. Which debt is causing you the most financial strain right now? What is your monthly debt payment amount, and how much more might you reasonably add to your priority payment? What action or event first led to your most needless debt? What can you do right now to stop that trend from happening again? When those commitments are removed, what would you do with the money that is now being used to pay off debt?

Financial freedom is not achieved in a single, dramatic event, but rather through a lengthy process. An obligation is lessened with each payment. Avoiding needless purchases safeguards future earnings. Progress is made with each extra sum applied to debt. Every lesson gained from previous borrowing experiences can help avoid future errors. Although it may seem slow at times, steady movement is more important than quickness.

Achieving a zero balance is not the best outcome of good debt management. It involves learning how to make financial decisions without letting needless commitments dictate your destiny. Income can start more effectively meeting current needs and future objectives once debt is under control. Savings can increase. Investments may become feasible. Decisions about careers can become more adaptable. Unexpected costs can become less of a threat. Individual decisions can be made more independently.

Start by being honest with the numbers. Recognize your debt, comprehend the associated charges, develop a repayment plan, safeguard necessities, and cease creating needless debt. Then carry on. Redirect payment to the next priority when one commitment expires. Maintain the habits that led to the progress even after the ultimate debt has been lowered or erased.

Repeated decisions that progressively give you more control over your resources are the foundation of financial independence. Your future does not have to be determined by debt. Financial opportunities can increase, and liabilities can decrease with awareness, self-control, patience, and a sensible payback plan. Every ethical choice you make moves you closer to a future where a larger portion of your income is allocated to your objectives rather than your past.

CHAPTER V

Increasing Your Income

Growing Earning Power

One of the most crucial things a young adult can do to have a safe and prosperous financial life is to increase their earning potential. The ability to raise income over time by acquiring useful skills, gaining experience, enhancing performance, seizing better opportunities, and adjusting to economic shifts is referred to as earning power. There is a limit to how much can be saved while income stays low, even though managing spending and saving money are crucial. A person who consistently increases their earning capacity makes greater space for investing, saving, handling obligations, and pursuing worthwhile objectives. Therefore, increasing earning power involves more than just earning more money. It involves increasing one's worth, competence, adaptability, and readiness to seize chances throughout life.

Young individuals sometimes start their careers with little money and little experience. Although this is typical, it shouldn't last forever. Early in a career, there are many opportunities to learn, try new things, hone abilities, and identify areas of strength. Even if a job isn't the person's ultimate professional choice, it can nevertheless offer valuable experience. Working with clients can help you improve your communication abilities. Organization can be enhanced by scheduling. Critical thinking can be strengthened by solving difficulties at work. Digital skills can be developed while working with technology. Leading a little project can help you hone your leadership abilities. When these experiences are acknowledged and purposefully cultivated, they contribute to an individual's increasing professional worth.

Developing talents that companies and customers truly value is one of the best methods to boost earning potential. Because many sectors rely on specific knowledge, technical talents can be especially helpful. Opportunities for increased income can be found in digital marketing, programming, data analysis, graphic design, accounting, project management, sales, cybersecurity, skilled crafts, and other specialized fields. But technical proficiency isn't always sufficient. Additionally, very important are communication, dependability, problem-solving, teamwork, negotiation, flexibility, and emotional intelligence are very important. Combining great interpersonal skills with technical proficiency can make a person more effective and, consequently, more appealing to clients and employers.

Although education can increase one's earning potential, it should be considered an investment rather than just a credential. While certificates, apprenticeships, vocational programs, online courses, seminars, mentorships, and independent study can be more suitable for other career pathways, formal degrees can be useful for others. The crucial question is whether learning is boosting access to opportunities and enhancing practical skills rather than just whether a person is accumulating credentials. A young adult should think about what skills will be acquired, how that skill is valued in the economy, what opportunities it can offer, and whether the anticipated financial reward justifies the expense before investing a large sum of money in school.

Another important factor in earning power is experience. Those who can show that they can use their knowledge in practical settings are frequently rewarded by employers. Internships, part-time jobs, freelance work, volunteer work, personal projects, apprenticeships, and small company ventures are all ways for a young adult to gain experience. Even before a person has amassed many years in a formal job, these experiences can produce proof of ability. A list of school credentials may not always convey skill as well as a portfolio of completed work. The objective is to go from knowledge to proficiency consistently.

Learning how to convey professional value is a crucial component of increasing earning power. Many people put forth a lot of effort yet find it difficult to articulate their contributions. An individual should be able to explain the issues they resolve, the duties they oversee, the advancements they make, and the outcomes they get. Rather than only stating that they work hard, they may describe how they decreased mistakes, enhanced customer satisfaction, finished projects quickly, boosted sales, streamlined a procedure, or assisted a team in achieving a goal. Applications for promotions, new jobs, freelancing contracts, and other chances can be strengthened by specific evidence, which also makes professional worth simpler to identify.

Earnings power can also be influenced via negotiations. A person may eventually have the chance to talk about pay, duties, perks, working conditions, or project costs as their abilities and experience grow. Without proof, negotiations should not be viewed as a demand for money. Supported by proven performance, market expertise, specialized talents, and quantifiable contributions, it works better. A young adult who is aware of their own worth can participate in these discussions with more assurance. Even if an employer is unable to raise pay right away, a conversation may highlight chances for more duties, training, career advancement, performance bonuses, or upcoming pay evaluations.

Avoiding career stagnation is another requirement for increasing earning power. Competitiveness can be progressively diminished by staying in the same role for years without picking up new skills. Consumer preferences vary, industries evolve, new jobs appear, and technologies advance. Today's extremely valuable ability could not be as significant tomorrow. A lifelong learner is better equipped to handle these shifts. It's not always necessary to return to school full-time in order to continue studying. Professional development can be facilitated by reading, practicing, going to training, researching industry advancements, picking the brains of seasoned professionals, and finishing real-world assignments.

Earning capacity can also be strengthened by having several sources of revenue. While freelance employment, consulting, tutoring, creative services, online enterprises, or other legal pursuits may generate extra options, a primary career may offer security. The goal shouldn't be to work nonstop without taking breaks. Alternatively, it is possible to build extra revenue around useful talents and free time carefully. A person may eventually find a bigger business opportunity if they use an existing skill to generate a small side income. However, extra work needs to be carefully considered to ensure that it doesn't negatively impact relationships, education, health, or success in the primary career.

Because opportunities frequently arise through relationships, networking is another important factor. Using others only for one's own benefit is not what networking entails. It entails establishing sincere professional connections founded on mutual support, respect, dependability, and learning. A promising opportunity can be suggested by a teacher. A previous coworker might be aware of a position. A client may be introduced to someone by a professional relationship. A mentor might offer guidance to avoid making a costly career error. Thus, sustaining positive connections and a solid reputation might develop into a significant source of financial capital.

When a larger salary is paired with sound financial practices, the relationship between earning power and wealth becomes particularly evident. Raising income can only lead to increased spending habits if money management is not improved. A person's financial stability may not significantly improve if they immediately increase their lifestyle expenses after receiving a raise. Conversely, a person who raises their income while keeping their spending acceptable might use the extra funds for long-term objectives, investments, debt reduction, emergency savings, and education. Increasing revenue is most effective when it is transformed into long-term financial advancement.

In the end, increasing earning potential is a lifetime endeavor. It is not necessary for a young adult to know precisely where a job will take them. Developing the habit of being more competent and valued over time is what counts. Every new ability, worthwhile experience, professional connection, accomplished endeavor, and lesson learned from failure might help create new chances in the future. The objective is to develop the ability to generate value and be fairly compensated for it rather than constantly chasing money. Increased income can lead to additional options, resilience, and independence when earning capacity increases in tandem with financial discipline. A person who consciously makes investments in their own growth is not just getting ready for a higher salary. They are strengthening the basis for long-term financial confidence, freedom, and opportunity.

Creating Extra Income

A person's ability to save, invest, handle unforeseen expenses, and accomplish significant financial goals might be hampered by relying just on one source of income, which is why generating additional income is crucial to developing financial strength. An extra source of income can give a young adult more freedom and possibilities to increase their financial security without relying only on a regular pay check. It's not always necessary to launch a big company or put in a lot of overtime to earn extra money. A practical talent, a modest service, a part-time job, freelancing employment, or any other activity that generates real value for others can be the starting point. The most crucial idea is to embrace extra income with responsibility, forethought, and a clear knowledge of how the funds will help more general financial objectives.

Finding opportunities, resources, talents, and expertise that may be transformed into value is the first step in generating additional revenue. Without realizing their financial potential, people frequently have skills that others are prepared to pay for. Additional income can come from writing, graphic design, photography, tutoring, cooking, fixing things, organizing data, producing digital products, running social media, translating, teaching, or helping with administrative tasks. A young adult can assess their own talents and think about what abilities help others. The likelihood of developing a sustained source of income increases with the strength of the relationship between an individual's talent and a true need.

One useful strategy for making extra money is freelancing. Rather than taking on a second traditional job, an individual might provide clients with certain services based on their availability and capacity. Because work may be done around an existing schedule, freelancing can offer flexibility. It still calls for professionalism, though. Clear communication, meeting deadlines, setting fair rates, maintaining quality, and maintaining accurate records of earnings and expenses are all necessary. When someone views the activity as a responsible financial opportunity rather than just as occasional spending money, extra revenue has value.

Another route may be offered by small business ventures. A young adult could make handcrafted goods, sell goods, cook, offer a specialized service, resell suitable commodities, or start a basic internet business. Before investing large sums of money, starting small can lower financial risk and provide you a chance to learn. Demand testing, understanding consumer preferences, cost calculations, and determining whether the activity can generate a respectable profit are all possible. Spending a lot of money on a firm just because entrepreneurship seems appealing shouldn't be the aim. Real demand, cost control, and the capacity to deliver something that customers truly appreciate are the foundations of a sustainable firm.

Additionally, digital options have given people new methods to make money. Freelance employment, instructional materials, digital goods, remote support, design services, and other acceptable activities can all be found online. When assessing internet income offers, young folks should exercise caution. It can be deceptive to promise easy profits, guaranteed income, or immediate wealth. Reliability typically necessitates hard work, practical skills, consistency, and the capacity to deliver real value. One should be aware of the risks involved and how the firm actually makes money before paying fees or investing money in an online opportunity.

Careful time management is also necessary to generate more revenue. If extra work takes up so much time that it interferes with relationships, principal employment, education, health, or other obligations, it may become counterproductive. The goal of additional income should be to improve financial conditions rather than put undue strain on oneself. One can ascertain the practical number of hours available and select options that fall within those constraints. Opportunities that demand many hours for very little return may be less desirable than those that offer fair compensation for the time involved. Thus, a key component of effective income planning is learning to assess time as a resource.

There should be a clear financial rationale for any additional revenue. If you don't have a plan, extra money can be easily spent on lifestyle items. A person may predetermine that a portion of their additional income will go toward investments, debt reduction, emergency savings, schooling, or a significant financial objective. This establishes a clear link between further work and long-term advancement. An individual who works as a freelancer, for instance, might allocate a percentage of their earnings to investments and an emergency fund. The precise distribution is determined by personal circumstances, but having a purpose increases the impact of increased income.

Reducing debt might be a particularly beneficial way to increase income. Because a large amount of future income is already allocated to interest and repayment, high-interest debt might impede financial advancement. An opportunity to expedite debt payments without lowering necessary living costs may arise from more income. Monthly cash flow may improve as debt declines, enabling the person to reallocate funds to investments and savings. In this sense, more revenue might start a domino effect whereby one financial development facilitates the next.

Financial resilience can also be enhanced by additional income. If their employment is discontinued or their income decreases, a person with a single source of income may face significant challenges. A secondary source of income can help during difficult times, but it might not be able to fully replace a primary pay check. When paired with emergency savings and prudent financial planning, this can be quite beneficial. Having several sources of income can increase flexibility and lessen reliance on a single source of funding.

Professional abilities can also be enhanced by earning extra money. A person may learn about sales, communication, customer service, marketing, negotiation, project management, budgeting, technology, or leadership through a side project. These abilities may also enhance performance in a primary career. An activity that starts out as a modest way to make extra money could later result in greater job prospects, business expansion, or a more valuable professional network. This implies that benefits from additional income can go beyond the actual money earned.

Another crucial factor is price. Sometimes people undervalue their job out of fear that clients won't accept higher charges. Pricing, however, ought to take into account the time, resources, knowledge, running expenses, and value of delivering a good or service. Even in situations where demand is high, charging too little can render an activity unsustainable. Prices should, however, continue to be fair given the market and the quality offered. Understanding how to compute expenses and establish reasonable prices is a crucial financial ability that can help with future business growth as well as personal income.

Maintaining records should not be disregarded. Expenses, payments, equipment, materials, transportation, platform fees, and other charges can all result in additional revenue. A person can ascertain whether an endeavor is truly profitable by maintaining precise records. Because the amount of money earned may be less than the expenses incurred in producing it, revenue by itself does not indicate profit. Maintaining accurate records might also make it simpler to comprehend financial performance and fulfill relevant tax obligations. Confusion can be avoided later if additional revenue is handled professionally from the start.

It's important to be patient when generating additional revenue. Not every opportunity will lead to success right away. A person might test a service and find that there isn't much demand, or they might require some time to improve their abilities before clients are prepared to pay more. Making more money is not impossible if you don't succeed in your first effort. It can offer insights into customer preferences, areas for talent development, and potentially more promising options. More income can be made more sustainable through experimentation, learning, and steady improvement.

Increasing financial capability and broadening future options are ultimately the goals of generating additional revenue. It can help a young adult save more quickly, pay off debt, make more consistent investments, get ready for significant life events, and become less reliant on a single source of income. The activity that generates the most revenue right away is not always the best strategy. It is the chance to make a fair wage while maintaining sustainability, legitimacy, and compatibility with significant obligations. A young adult can transform extra income into a potent weapon for long-term financial advancement by finding useful abilities, solving actual issues, carefully managing time, controlling costs, keeping correct records, and allocating additional earnings toward meaningful financial goals. An extra source of income has the potential to grow beyond a short-term financial boost over time. It can help people become more independent, more resilient, and have more possibilities in the future.

Improving Career Value

One of the most crucial ways a young adult can improve their financial security and future prospects is to increase the value of their career. The combination of information, abilities, experience, relationships, and traits that make a person competitive and helpful in the job is referred to as career value. Strong career values increase a person's chances of being hired for better positions, earning more money, getting promoted, and being able to adjust with the times. Developing a valuable career takes time. Understanding one's own talents is the first step in this ongoing process, which also involves learning useful skills, gaining experience, taking on responsibilities, and continuing to strive for improvement. The objective is to become someone whose skills constantly add value for an employer, a customer, a team, or a business, rather than just finding a job.

Young adults frequently undervalue the financial benefits of advancing their jobs. They could place a lot of emphasis on preserving little sums of money while ignoring the possibility that improving earning capacity can have a considerably greater long-term impact on financial advancement. While saving is vital, income is what makes it feasible to save, invest, pay off debt, and make other financial decisions. A person can build a stronger financial foundation by increasing their earning potential while upholding prudent spending practices. For instance, a young worker may eventually have more money available for emergency savings, retirement investments, schooling, or business chances if they acquire specialized skills and earn a better wage. Because better professional skills can result in better income opportunities, career growth becomes a component of financial planning.

Determining which abilities are useful in the chosen area is the first step toward increasing career worth. Employers seek a mix of technical and interpersonal skills in all professions. Computer expertise, data analysis, writing, accounting, design, programming, sales, marketing, project management, and equipment operation are examples of technical talents. Reliability in communication, teamwork, problem-solving, organization, flexibility, and emotional control are examples of personal skills. Young individuals should look at job descriptions in the field they want to work in and note which talents are frequently mentioned. This can highlight the skills that employers value. A person might choose a few high-value talents and consciously develop them through classes, practice projects, reading, mentoring, and actual professional experience rather than attempting to acquire everything at once.

When education is linked to practical competence, it can make a substantial contribution to professional worth. While a certificate, degree, workshop, or training program can show dedication and offer helpful information, qualifications by themselves do not ensure success in the workplace. Additionally, employers seek proof that an individual can put what they have learned into practice. By developing projects, finishing internships, volunteering for duties, engaging in professional activities, or accepting assignments that offer quantifiable experience, a young adult can increase the value of their career. For instance, someone with an interest in marketing could work on developing promotional materials, studying consumer behavior, or running a small social media campaign. A tech enthusiast could create straightforward websites or data initiatives. These encounters produce proof of skill and enhance the significance of professional discussions.

Another important component of professional value is communication, since even highly skilled individuals may find it difficult to collaborate with others or adequately explain concepts. Effective communication is paying close attention, posing insightful questions, crafting clear messages, confidently presenting information, and modifying communication based on the audience. With regular practice, young adults can enhance these skills. They can learn how to engage politely in meetings, write professional emails, clarify issues without needless confusion, and give concise updates on their work. Knowing when to talk and when to listen is another aspect of effective communication. Reliable communication makes a person easier to trust and collaborate with, which can lead to more opportunities for more responsibility.

Another crucial professional quality is reliability. People who arrive on time, meet deadlines, own up to mistakes, and finish tasks without continual monitoring are highly valued by employers. Impressive skills are not the sole factor that determines a career's worth. Professional activity that is repeated over time also shapes it. A young adult might establish a reputation for dependability by continuously producing high-quality work. Eventually, that reputation might result in more duties, recommendations, promotions, or possibilities that less dependable employees wouldn't have access to right now. A strong professional reputation can be gradually built by small behaviors like maintaining promises, planning assignments, reacting promptly, and reviewing work before submitting.

Because industries and workplaces are always changing, adaptability is particularly crucial. Employers may alter the skills they require, firms may modify their plans, and technology creates new tools. When a single ability loses value, a person who relies only on it may become vulnerable. A person can react more skillfully if they cultivate a learning mentality. Young individuals might see new technology, new responsibilities, and unexpected work as chances to develop their skills rather than as obstacles to change. Because it enables a person to continue growing throughout their working life, learning how to learn may turn out to be one of the most important career abilities.

Because professional chances frequently arise through contacts and reputation, networking can also increase the worth of a career. Asking everyone for a job is not the definition of networking. It entails establishing sincere business connections with those who have similar interests or operate in comparable sectors. Teachers, coworkers, managers, professional associations, mentors, and seasoned people are all accessible to young adults. Speaking with informed individuals can uncover career paths, abilities, industry expectations, and opportunities that might not be apparent from the outside. When making tough job decisions, a solid network can also offer guidance. When relationships are built on respect, generosity, dependability, and mutual support rather than on instant personal gain, they become more precious.

Learning to gauge professional advancement is a crucial component of increasing career worth. A person should regularly review the lessons they have learned, the tasks they have completed, and the outcomes they have achieved. It is more beneficial to list particular achievements rather than just stating that they worked hard. Practical value can be demonstrated by finishing a project, enhancing a procedure, boosting sales, decreasing errors, assisting clients in resolving challenging issues, or training a new employee. Because the person can clearly articulate contributions, keeping a record of successes can improve the effectiveness of future job applications, interviews, performance reviews, and wage conversations.

When someone gains both professional skill and financial understanding, their career value also rises. Increased income may not always translate into riches. Financial progress may be constrained if income rises at the same rate as consumption. Therefore, young adults should make the connection between good money management and job growth. The extra cash from a promotion or better job might be purposefully allocated to living expenditures, debt reduction, investments, and personal objectives. Instead of only generating chances for increased spending, this strategy enables career advancement to assist broader financial progress.

Since professional development is typically gradual, increasing career worth needs patience. A person may start off with little money and little expertise, but with persistent work, they can increase their worth. A firmer professional foundation is the result of every practical skill acquired, every responsibility taken on, every error fixed, and every relationship formed. The most effective strategy is to concentrate on improving one's abilities rather than continuously comparing one's progress to that of others. When career growth is viewed as a long-term investment in one's ability to make money, it becomes more potent.

In the end, boosting professional value entails developing one's ability, usefulness, adaptability, and reliability. It entails realizing that a career is an asset that can be developed consciously rather than just a source of monthly revenue. Young adults can expand their chances and improve their capacity to manage financial responsibilities by investing in their skills. Individuals who disregard professional growth may continue to rely on scarce opportunities and become more susceptible to shifts in the economy. A young adult can produce higher professional worth and convert that value into better income potential, greater financial flexibility, and a more secure future by continuously learning, enhancing communication, gaining experience, building relationships, and exhibiting dependability.

Professional Growth

Increasing your income is important because financial advancement depends not only on prudent money management but also on the power to generate additional revenue over time. Even if someone learns to be frugal with their spending and saving, a low income may still limit the speed at which significant objectives can be accomplished. Gaining professional worth can open doors to better positions, more stable employment, higher compensation, and extra revenue streams. This is particularly crucial for young adults since early professional choices can have long-term effects on earning potential. When professional growth concepts are applied, the focus shifts from how to make ends meet with current income to how to increase one's value in the marketplace in the future. It promotes ongoing education, the development of useful skills, improved communication, improved productivity, and deliberate career choices.

The benefits of ongoing professional development can go beyond a higher salary. A higher salary can free up more funds for investment, debt reduction, saving, education, family obligations, and personal objectives. Additionally, having more money can give you more flexibility in the event of unforeseen events. A person who has acquired useful skills might have more options for where to work, what possibilities to take advantage of, and how to bargain for pay. Thus, both financial and personal freedom can be achieved with professional advancement. Making more money is not the only goal. It is to cultivate the capacity to produce value and be fairly compensated for it.

Neglecting professional development can have a slow but profound effect. Opportunities may go unrecognized, earning potential may stagnate, and skills may become outdated. Years of hard work may result in little financial advancement if skill development and smart career planning are not integrated with the effort. While it may seem safe to stay in a comfortable position, comfort can become costly if it stunts growth. Because it manifests as income that was never earned rather than money that was explicitly lost, the cost of neglecting professional development is sometimes unseen.

Regular career decisions demonstrate the practical effects of professional development. Imagine a young worker who doesn't acquire new abilities and completes the same tasks every year. Another employee in the same company gains specialized knowledge, volunteers for difficult projects, learns new technologies, and enhances communication skills. After a few years, the second employee could be able to get better jobs and more money because their value has grown. Even though they both put in a lot of effort, one has consciously expanded their professional capabilities.

By the end of this chapter, you will be able to pinpoint the skills that will make you more valuable in your present or intended career, design a workable development plan that links education with more lucrative opportunities, and take intentional action to increase your income through career advancement, negotiating, taking on more work, or other fruitful opportunities. These results are intended to make professional development more than just a theoretical concept. Finding what the market values, developing those skills, showcasing them well, and using the ensuing value to generate better financial prospects are the goals.

A real-world example is a young administrative employee who wishes to boost their revenue despite receiving a meager salary. The employee looks at job postings for higher-level administrative roles and finds that many of them demand spreadsheet abilities, project coordination, digital communication, and basic data analysis, rather than immediately looking for a whole different career. Through actual job assignments and reasonably priced learning resources, the employee choose one skill at a time to develop. After a few months, the employee is able to show off their improved skills and applies for jobs with more responsibility. The key takeaway is that income growth frequently starts before compensation increases. It starts when someone consciously cultivates skills that enable a greater degree of involvement.

This approach is demonstrated using a short narrative. Luis, a young man, appreciated his job, but he was dissatisfied because his pay had hardly altered. At first, he thot that getting a new job was the only way to solve the problem. He looked at job descriptions for professions he wanted before departing and found that he lacked a number of critical abilities. He started learning those talents in his spare time and sought chances to put them into practice at work. Eventually, he offered to take on a project that called for his recently acquired skills. After noticing the progress, his management assigned him more tasks. Luis thereafter applied for a more senior role and was given a pay raise. The elevation was not the beginning of his greatest transformation. It started when he began preparing for the chance instead of waiting for it.

Considering professional talents as tools in a toolbox is a helpful metaphor. A worker may be able to finish routine jobs with just a few basic tools, but their options may be limited when more complicated work comes up. A worker can manage a wider variety of issues and offer more value if they consistently add helpful tools. A person can explore more opportunities if they have a stronger collection of applicable abilities, but each new skill does not ensure a higher salary. Thus, developing professionally is similar to adding more tools to your toolbox. You can tackle more valuable problems if you create more useful tools.

The Value Growth Cycle is a straightforward structure that might offer a quick route ahead. Observe is the first step. Examine your current position, your industry, and the kinds of jobs you want to pursue. Determine the abilities that clients, employers, and consumers regularly value. Select is the second step. Select one or two abilities that will increase your earning potential and are feasible to acquire. Practice is the third step. Instead of depending solely on theory, apply those abilities in practical settings. Demonstrate is the fourth step. Use finished projects, quantifiable outcomes, portfolios, certifications, recommendations, or professional accomplishments to demonstrate your abilities. Leverage is the fifth phase. Utilize your increased worth to seek more responsibility, haggle over pay, apply for more secure jobs, locate clients, or create new revenue streams. Repeat is the sixth step. Repeat the loop after determining the next helpful ability.

Random learning is prevented by the Observe phase. Young folks frequently spend time learning about a wide range of topics without becoming experts in fields that directly affect their employment prospects. When learning is linked to real-world needs, professional growth is more successful. Examine job postings, talk to seasoned professionals, look at typical requirements, and research what accomplished individuals in your preferred industry are capable of. You can use this information to find abilities that are useful in real-world situations.

Focus is needed during the Select stage. It can be frustrating to try to learn everything at once. Select abilities that enhance your current knowledge and are feasible to acquire in the time you have available. Instead of beginning with an unconnected ability that has no clear connection to future chances, a person working in customer service, for instance, might learn sales communication, digital marketing, data management, or team coordination.

Knowledge becomes ability in the Practice stage. Understanding can be gained by watching lessons or reading material, but application is the key to developing true competency. Participate in a project as a volunteer, make a sample project, practice in real-world scenarios, help an experienced person, or apply the skill in your present position. The objective is to go from understanding a skill to being able to use it to achieve beneficial outcomes.

It is common to forget the Demonstrate step. When evidence of a skill is visible to others, it gains value. If you become more adept at analyzing data, present the findings. Make samples of your work if you are learning design. If you become a better leader, keep a record of the projects you assisted in planning and the outcomes attained. Employers, clients, or business partners can more easily perceive your professional value if you have evidence.

Development turns into financial advancement at the leverage stage. Once you've developed practical talents, seek ways to make more money with them. This could entail asking for more work, applying for a promotion, switching jobs, negotiating pay, taking on freelancing work, creating a service, or considering starting your own business. While skill development can still be beneficial even in the absence of financial application, the effort is strengthened when skills are linked to opportunities.

Communication is also necessary for professional development. Being competent is crucial, but others must recognize the value you offer. Develop a concise explanation of your achievements. Describe the issue, the solution, and the outcome rather than just stating that you finished a project. These results offer significant proof of your impact if you were able to lower errors, save time, boost customer satisfaction, enhance organization, or raise income.

Additionally, it is important to approach income negotiations as a professional discussion rather than a personal demand. Evidence backs up effective negotiating. Examine the role's worth, recognize your achievements, list any new tasks you have taken on, and explain your potential contribution. The discussion might highlight the abilities or outcomes needed for future progress, even in cases where an immediate gain is not feasible.

Professional development can be enhanced by additional revenue, but it must be handled wisely. A side project shouldn't be used as a justification for working nonstop or ignoring other obligations. The most long-term supplemental income frequently builds on abilities you already have or are learning. Existing skills can occasionally be transformed into added value in a variety of fields, including writing, design, tutoring, consulting, technical services, sales, digital work, and small business operations.

Long-term success-influencing personal traits should be included in professional development. Others' perceptions of your professional worth can be influenced by your dependability, communication, problem-solving skills, flexibility, emotional maturity, time management, and openness to learning. While dependable behavior can help you continue to advance once you have an opportunity, technical skills may help you get it.

It's also crucial to refrain from thinking that having more money makes you wealthy. If spending increases at the same rate, a gain in compensation may swiftly vanish. Financial foundations should be strengthened in part when professional development results in increased revenue. More funds can be allocated to better living conditions, debt repayment, savings, investments, education, and worthwhile experiences. Allowing higher income to produce long-term financial gains as opposed to transient lifestyle inflation is the aim.

This lesson can be put into practice with the use of reflection questions. Which ability might increase your value in your intended or present career? What proof do you have that you have mastered this ability? If your skills developed over the course of the next year, what career opportunity would you be able to pursue? Instead of just raising your spending, how can you use higher income to improve your financial future? What particular steps can you take this week to start learning a talent that can help you make more money?

Growing professionally is a continuous process. Technology advances, customer demands alter, industries shift, and new opportunities arise. It's possible that the abilities that add value now won't do so in a few years. By consistently questioning what is changing, what people need, and what skills can assist in meeting those requirements, a lifelong learner maintains their adaptability.

The most crucial change is to cease considering income as a set amount. The value of your existing situation, abilities, experience, obligations, and possibilities is reflected in your current income. It doesn't always dictate your future earning potential. You can expand your options by acquiring useful skills and learning how to express and use them.

Start by assessing your current situation. Decide where you wish to go. Examine the abilities needed to get there. Select a worthwhile skill, practice it regularly, show off your abilities, and find methods to turn that development into an opportunity. After that, keep learning. Each practical ability becomes an additional tool in your professional toolkit.

Greater competence lays the groundwork for earning that income, but higher income might lead to more options. Career advancement becomes more deliberate when professional development becomes a regular practice. Waiting for someone else to see your potential is no longer your only option. You can deliberately cultivate the traits, abilities, and outcomes that increase the value of your contribution.

The decisions you make today regarding your ability might strengthen your financial future. Learn with purpose, practice regularly, show your worth, and seek out situations that showcase your developing skills. However, it could take some time; every new ability you acquire broadens your capabilities, and every practical experience enhances your offerings. Therefore, increasing one's income is not the only way to advance professionally. It is about developing the ability to generate more value, gain access to better possibilities, and use higher earning power to construct a more robust and adaptable future.

CHAPTER VI

Starting Smart Investing

Investment Foundations

Understanding that investing is a long-term financial activity intended to help money grow and support future goals is the first step in understanding investment foundations. Learning the fundamentals of investing can be quite beneficial for young adults because investments and their potential returns can compound over time. Investing shouldn't be seen as a means of making quick money or as a kind of gamble based on short-term price fluctuations and rumors. Financial literacy, reasonable expectations, disciplined saving, sensible risk management, and a firm grasp of one's own objectives are the first steps toward a solid investing foundation.

A person should have a solid financial basis prior to investing. Investing can be made more sustainable with consistent income, controllable spending, emergency reserves, and prudent debt management. Because the value of investments might change, having an emergency fund is crucial. A person without accessible funds might have to sell at a bad moment if an unforeseen expense arises when investments have decreased. Therefore, increasing stability can be achieved by building a financial buffer prior to taking on major investment risk. Expensive debt should also be taken into account because paying high interest rates could yield a more assured financial gain than taking on more investment risk.

Another crucial basis is knowing how risk and return are related. Increased risk and potential loss are typically associated with investments that have the potential for larger returns. Although their prospective returns may be smaller, safer assets can be crucial for preserving stability and safeguarding funds. Young investors should be aware that there is no risk-free investment that will guarantee large profits. Promises of very high earnings with minimal or no risk must be handled with caution. Investors might avoid making decisions based on irrational expectations by learning to assess risk.

When developing an investment strategy, time horizon is equally crucial. In general, funds meant for a long-term objective shouldn't be subject to the same degree of investment volatility as funds needed in the near future. A large market decrease could cause problems if money is needed shortly for a big purchase. Long-term investments might have more time to recover from short-term market swings. Knowing when funds will be required aids in determining the proper level of risk. Because every investment choice is linked to a particular financial goal, investing becomes more meaningful as a result.

Another key idea is diversification. If a person invests all of their money in a single business, sector, or asset, they run the risk of suffering large losses if that investment underperforms. One way to lessen reliance on a single source of return is through asset diversification. Risk is not eliminated by diversification, and the value of a diversified portfolio may still decrease. Spreading investments, however, might lessen the impact of issues with a certain asset. This idea may be taught to young adults at a young age, and they can use it as their financial portfolio grows in size and complexity.

It's also helpful to comprehend fundamental investment classifications. Although they can offer prospective growth and occasionally dividends, stocks represent ownership interests in businesses and are subject to large price fluctuations. Although bonds have risks including interest rate and credit risk, they typically reflect providing money to an issuer in exchange for interest and repayment under predetermined terms. Funds may make diversification easier by exposing investors to groupings of investments. Although real estate entails significant expenses and obligations, it may offer prospective income or gain. No single asset is always suitable for every investor, and each category has unique qualities.

Because fees and expenses can eventually lower investment returns, they should be carefully considered. Depending on the investment, expenses could include commissions, account fees, transaction costs, management fees, and other expenditures. When a price is charged regularly over a long period of time, it can seem insignificant at first. Young investors should be taught to look at an investment's overall cost and comprehend what they are getting in return. Although excessive expenses might lower the amount of money available for long-term growth, lower costs do not always equate to better.

One of the most effective ideas in investing is compounding. Investment profits have the potential to produce more profits in the future if they are kept invested. This procedure can greatly raise the value of regular contributions over extended periods of time. There may be more time for compounding to take effect the earlier a person starts forming disciplined investment habits. This does not imply that all investments will increase steadily or that losses will never happen. Rather, it illustrates the significance of persistence and patience in long-term investing.

Emotional control is also necessary for a solid investment basis. Rapid market growth can thrill investors and motivate them to take unwarranted risks. They may also drastically decrease, which would be frightening and unsettling. Buying after prices have significantly increased or selling after prices have decreased can result from emotionally reacting to every market action. It can be simpler to stay focused if you have a clear financial plan in place before these circumstances arise. Frequent evaluations can lessen needless responses to temporary adjustments while assisting in determining whether the plan still aligns with individual objectives.

Investing habits can also be strengthened by consistent donations. Rather than attempting to find the ideal moment to invest, one may set up a regular timeframe for making financial contributions. This strategy promotes self-control and normalizes investing as a component of money management. As income rises, the amount may also rise. Although it can lessen reliance on having one ideal market choice, consistent investing does not ensure rewards. The main takeaway is that consistent excellent habits are frequently more important for long-term financial success than sporadic bold decisions.

Maintaining personal objectives is another aspect of investment foundations. Investing for a short-term purchase is not the same as investing for retirement. A person generating long-term wealth may have a different time horizon and risk tolerance than someone saving for school. Determining how much risk may be justified and how long the money can be invested is made easier by clearly defining the goal of the investment. Additionally, goals serve as a source of inspiration when things seem to be moving slowly.

Another crucial pillar is ongoing education. Investment knowledge should progressively grow via trustworthy sources and thorough research. Asset allocation, diversification, inflation, taxes, fees, market cycles, and other investment products may all be learned. Predicting every market action or becoming an expert overnight are not the objectives. The goal is to get sufficient knowledge to identify potentially hazardous promises and make well-informed decisions. Asking better questions when seeking assistance is another benefit of financial knowledge.

In the end, preparation, knowledge, discipline, and patience are the building blocks of solid investment foundations. A young adult can build a stronger foundation for long-term investing by setting up emergency savings, managing costly debt, comprehending risk, identifying financial goals, learning about various investment types, diversifying appropriately, controlling costs, making consistent contributions, and avoiding emotional decisions. Selecting an asset is only one aspect of investing. It involves developing a financial procedure that can be adhered to in the face of shifting market conditions and life stages. Money has a better chance of supporting long-term wealth growth, financial independence, and future goals when investing is integrated into a larger financial strategy.

Choosing Investments

Making wise investment decisions is crucial to building long-term financial confidence because investing allows money to grow beyond what regular saving can. The first step in the process for a young adult should be realizing that investing is not about getting rich quickly. It involves making deliberate financial decisions that are not urgently required and letting time, consistency, and prudent risk-taking cooperate. Every investment choice should have a specific financial goal in mind. While some invest for retirement, others do so for long-term financial independence, a future home, education, or business opportunities. It is easier to decide how much risk is acceptable, how long the money can be invested, and what kinds of investments might be appropriate when one knows why the money is being invested. Without a clear goal, it is simple to follow trends, respond emotionally to shifts in the market, or make investment decisions just because it seems like other people are profiting from them.

The connection between risk and potential return is among the first concepts to comprehend. Higher potential returns on investments are frequently accompanied by increased risk of loss and uncertainty. Lower-risk investments typically offer fewer opportunities for significant growth, but they may yield more predictable results. Because there is plenty of time to recover from losses, a young investor shouldn't assume that taking the biggest risk is always the best option. Rather, risk should be evaluated in light of individual circumstances, financial obligations, expertise, and investment objectives. A person may be able to withstand more market fluctuation than someone who needs the money soon if they have a steady income, emergency savings, manageable debt, and many years before they need the invested money. Knowing one's own risk tolerance aids in avoiding choices that might cause needless financial strain.

Understanding the main investment categories is a crucial component of making investment decisions. In addition to representing ownership in businesses, stocks can generate growth through value increases and, occasionally, dividend payments. Bonds typically entail lending money to a business, government, or other entity in return for interest and repayment under predetermined conditions. Gaining exposure to a variety of assets without having to choose each individual security is made possible by mutual funds and exchange-traded funds, which can hold collections of various investments. Investing in real estate can also be profitable, but it frequently necessitates larger sums of money, continuous management, and awareness of regional market conditions. Investments in cash and cash equivalents may offer more stability and simpler access to funds, but their potential for growth may be constrained. Young adults should understand how an investment operates before making a financial commitment because each category has unique features, costs, risks, and potential rewards.

Another idea that can help investors make more balanced choices is diversification. Spreading money over a variety of investments rather than heavily depending on a single business, sector, asset class, or market is known as diversification. Other investments could lessen the impact on the portfolio as a whole if one investment does poorly. A diversified portfolio may still experience a decline during a general market downturn because diversification does not completely eliminate losses. On the other hand, it can lessen the risk of having an excessively reliant financial future on a single investment. Therefore, rather than trying to guess which one investment will do the best, a young investor can concentrate on creating a portfolio that is sufficiently diverse to reflect various opportunities.

Because small fees can have a big impact over many years, investment costs also need to be carefully considered. Account fees, transaction fees, management fees, and other costs are associated with certain investments. Recurring expenses can lower the amount available for future growth when money is invested for decades. Investors can avoid paying needlessly high costs by learning to compare fees and comprehend the services being offered. It is not necessary for a young adult to select an investment just because it is well-known or heavily promoted. The crucial inquiry is whether the price is fair in light of the investment plan and anticipated returns.

The process of choosing investments should include research as well. Prior to making an investment, one should be aware of the investment's contents, potential returns, risks, fees, and situations in which it might depreciate. Reliable financial data is more valuable than rumors, claims made on social media, or assurances of profits. Even if an investment seems exciting, it might not be the right choice. Young adults are especially susceptible to rapidly spreading financial trends on the internet, particularly when people highlight spectacular success stories without outlining the associated risks or losses. Patience and a readiness to challenge claims that seem too good to be true are necessary for responsible investing.

One of the biggest advantages for a young investor is time. Starting earlier can give investments more chances to profit from compound growth, which is the process by which returns on an investment can produce additional returns. This does not imply that investment outcomes are assured. Losses and market fluctuations are possible. Instead of being compelled to sell during a bad time, a long investment horizon can offer more opportunities to stay invested through brief declines. Therefore, having more money now is not the only benefit of starting early. The idea is to give financial growth more time to mature.

Emotional self-control is just as crucial. Investment markets can arouse fear when prices decline and excitement when they rise. Investors may buy without a plan out of fear of missing out or sell out of fear of short-term losses. Long-term objectives may be hampered by these responses. Instead of continuously responding to changes in the market, a thoughtful investor develops a strategy before feelings become strong and reviews it on a regular basis. This strategy promotes patience and aids in distinguishing a well-thought-out financial plan from transient market noise.

In the end, making an investment choice should be seen as a continuous learning process rather than a single choice. As income, obligations, family situations, and priorities change, so do financial goals. A suitable investment strategy at one point in life might need to be modified at a later time. To make sure the portfolio still fits the investor's objectives, time horizon, risk tolerance, and financial circumstances, it can be helpful to review investments on a regular basis. However, making unneeded changes on a regular basis can lead to extra expenses and emotional decision-making. The objective is to stay conscious and deliberate rather than to adapt constantly.

Successful investing for a young adult starts with preparation, knowledge, and reasonable expectations. Before taking big investment risks, a stronger foundation can be created by creating an emergency fund, controlling high-cost debt, developing regular saving habits, and comprehending personal financial objectives. Investments can become a tool for long-term growth and increased financial flexibility once that foundation is established. The most important lesson is that excitement, popularity, or the prospect of quick profits should never be the only factors considered when making investment decisions. Understanding risk, diversifying wisely, keeping expenses under control, doing thorough research, and exercising patience are all necessary for making wise investment decisions. Investing becomes less about chasing opportunities and more about purposefully creating a financial future through consistent, well-informed decision-making when these habits are formed early.

Building Investment Habits

Since effective investing is typically not predicated on making a single, flawless choice, cultivating investment habits is crucial to building long-term financial strength. It is developed via consistent behavior, perseverance, self-control, and an openness to learning. Early investment habits can be advantageous for a young adult since compound interest permits money to increase over time. The objective is not to pursue assets that promise quick gains or to get wealthy right away. Rather, the objective is to develop a consistent strategy that can be upheld during all phases of life. Knowing why investing is important, knowing what one wants to achieve, and establishing a routine that makes investing a regular aspect of money management are the first steps in developing a good investment habit.

Investing regularly instead of waiting for the ideal opportunity is one of the best habits. Many people put off investing because they think they need a sizable sum of money before they can start. In actuality, cultivating the habit of consistently putting money aside is more crucial. A person might become accustomed to the practice with even a small investment made on a regular basis. Contributions on a regular basis can help lessen the temptation to spend every peso that is available. Investing can be given the same consideration as rent, food, transportation, savings, or other essential costs when it is incorporated into a monthly financial routine. Contributions should be made consistently, but the amount may rise as income does.

Paying yourself first is another beneficial practice. This is determining ahead of time how much money should be allocated to future financial objectives and putting that sum away before needless expenditures occur. When a young adult gets paid, they might instantly consider entertainment, shopping, dining, subscriptions, or other purchases. There might not be much left over for future objectives in the absence of a conscious plan. Priorities are rearranged when investments are made first. After taking into account necessary financial responsibilities and suitable cash reserves, an individual can devote a predetermined amount toward investments rather than investing whatever happens to be left at the end of the month. Because planned transfers can eliminate the need to make the same decision repeatedly, automation can facilitate this process.

Learning is a habit that must be developed in order to build investment habits. Before making an investment, people should be aware of the dangers involved. Young investors might study exchange-traded funds, equities, bonds, mutual funds, retirement accounts, real estate, and other investing strategies. Additionally, they can learn about compound growth, fees, risk tolerance, time horizon, diversification, and inflation. Predicting every market action is not the goal of learning. For a variety of reasons, markets can fluctuate, and even seasoned investors are unable to forecast short-term shifts reliably. Instead, financial education enables a person to make decisions based on information rather than social pressure, excitement, fear, or hearsay.

Keeping emotional responses and economic decisions apart is a particularly crucial habit. Both periods of rapid collapse and periods of robust expansion are possible for financial markets. An investor may get overconfident and wish to take excessive risks as their investments appreciate in value. The same investor can panic and sell when prices decline without thinking about the investment's initial goal. Creating a long-term strategy might lessen these emotional responses. A person may be more equipped to maintain patience amid brief market fluctuations if they comprehend the rationale behind an investment's selection and how it fits into a larger strategy. Being emotionally disciplined does not entail ignoring real issues. It entails carefully assessing developments rather than letting enthusiasm or fear dictate every choice.

Another practice that can improve an investment regimen is diversification. A person may be exposed to needless risk if they invest all of their available funds in a single business, sector, or kind of asset. One way to lessen the impact of a bad outcome in one area is to diversify your investments. To exercise diversification, a young adult does not necessarily need a complex portfolio. Avoiding being reliant on a single investment for future financial success is a crucial lesson. Additionally, diversification should take into account one's time horizon, financial objectives, personal situation, and readiness to bear investment losses.

Periodically reviewing investments is also beneficial, but doing so all the time might be detrimental. An individual who checks investment prices on a daily basis may experience anxiety and be more prone to rash actions. Setting aside appropriate times to examine the overall strategy is a healthier habit. An investor can assess if contributions are still acceptable, whether financial objectives have changed, whether the portfolio is still fairly diversified, and whether fees or other expenses are having an impact on outcomes. Reviewing does not include buying and selling all the time. In many situations, carrying out the current plan could be the most beneficial course of action.

Good spending practices are linked to good investment practices. Basic financial stability shouldn't be sacrificed for investing. Before making an ambitious investment, a young adult should think about high-cost debt, emergency funds, and other significant financial obligations. Because unforeseen costs are less likely to drive someone to sell investments at an inconvenient moment, having a solid financial base might make it simpler to stay invested during trying times. This proves that investing is not a solitary endeavor. It functions best when integrated within a comprehensive financial system that also includes long-term planning, income creation, appropriate borrowing, budgeting, saving, and emergency financial protection.

Another strong habit is to increase investing contributions as income increases. It can be tempting to instantly raise lifestyle spending when someone earns a bonus, salary increase, freelancing income, or other additional revenue. Alternatively, some of the extra funds could be used for investments. This makes it possible to advance financially without drastically lowering present living standards. Gradually raising contributions can have a significant impact on the total amount spent over time. Instead of letting every increase in income vanish through increased expenditure, it's important to make increases deliberate.

Maintaining documentation can help reinforce investment discipline. Contributions, account balances, fees, investment goals, and significant choices can all be monitored by an investor. The goal is to keep a clear picture of development rather than becoming fixated on daily shifts in value. Records can also be used to identify behavioral trends. Someone may find that contributions ceased whenever unanticipated expenditure surged, or that investments were frequently altered during times of market volatility. Acknowledging these trends offers a chance to get better. Finding minor flaws and developing processes that facilitate better decision-making are often the first steps toward financial advancement.

One of the most crucial investing skills a young adult can acquire is probably patience. Generally speaking, accumulating wealth takes time. When money is invested and has enough time to grow, compounding works best. This implies that the initial phases may seem sluggish at times. For months or years, a person may make financial contributions without experiencing noticeable outcomes. That does not imply that the procedure is not working. Because they lay the groundwork for future development, the early years are important. As income and investment balances increase, the habit of continuing to contribute, learning from experience, controlling risk, and avoiding needless speculation can become more and more useful.

In the end, developing investment habits is more about developing a system that can be repeated than it is about looking for the ideal investment. Financial behaviors that can last for decades are being developed by a young adult who learns to invest regularly, save before spending, comprehend risk, diversify correctly, control emotional reactions, frequently check progress, raise contributions as income grows, and maintain patience. Having an investment account is not the most significant accomplishment. It involves developing the ability to carefully handle finances and make future-focused judgments. Investing becomes a regular aspect of financial life when one has sound investment habits. Small financial acts can progressively grow into a significant foundation for long-term prosperity and increased financial freedom with self-control, education, perseverance, and consistency.

Beginning Your Wealth Building

It's crucial to start investing because creating financial security involves more than just earning and spending money. While investing allows suitable long-term funds to grow and possibly generate additional wealth, saving offers a crucial foundation. This can be particularly significant for a young adult since time can turn into a valuable financial resource. Money can potentially benefit from growth and compounding over a longer period of time if one starts with reasonable amounts and maintains consistent habits. The goal is not to become wealthy fast or to accurately forecast market movements. The goal is to create a methodical strategy that links money now with worthwhile financial opportunities later on.

A person's perspective on money starts to shift when they use smart investing. Money is no longer only thot of as something that can be saved or spent. Certain funds can be used effectively to achieve long-term objectives. Increased patience and decisions based on long-term requirements rather than short-term thrills can result from this. If a young adult starts making wise investments, they might eventually have money for retirement, schooling, a house, starting their own business, taking care of their family, or having more freedom. The expansion of an investment account is not the only significant change. It is the cultivation of a long-term financial perspective.

Ignoring investments can also have negative effects. It is possible for someone to earn and save for many years without realizing how assets can help with future financial growth. Long-term growth prospects may be postponed, and inflation may progressively lower purchasing power. In order to accomplish some goals, waiting until later in life may also necessitate greater contributions. Avoiding investing is not the only risk, though. Uninformed investing can be just as harmful. Unnecessary losses can result from following unreliable advice, chasing trends, concentrating money on a single opportunity, or expecting guaranteed returns. Therefore, both action and caution are necessary for smart investing.

When investing is linked to a particular goal, its effects on real life become more apparent. During the first few months, a young person who makes regular investments for a far-off goal might not notice significant changes. However, consistent contributions and possible investment growth can add up to significant resources over a long period of time. Additionally, the process can foster beneficial financial discipline. The investor learns to consistently use a manageable amount of money rather than waiting for a substantial sum to appear. As income rises, this habit may intensify.

By the end of this chapter, you will be able to assess whether your current financial situation is suitable for long-term investing, select an investment strategy that aligns with your time horizon and risk tolerance, and create a regular investing schedule that facilitates the steady accumulation of wealth. These skills make investing a conscious process as opposed to a response to market excitement. Understanding why you are investing, what you are investing in, the risks you are taking, and how the strategy fits into your larger financial life are all important.

A young worker with a steady salary, controllable spending, emergency savings, and no pressing high-cost debt is a good example. The employee first establishes a long-term goal and calculates how much money can be invested reasonably, rather than investing all available savings in a popular asset because someone online promises quick profits. The employee researches various investment options, weighs costs and diversification, and chooses a strategy suitable for the targeted time frame. Then, while short-term market fluctuations are viewed patiently, contributions are made consistently. While pursuing quick profits may seem more thrilling, this strategy builds a more sustainable system.

This is important, and it can be illustrated with a brief story. After receiving her first regular salary, a young woman named Anna wanted to accumulate wealth as soon as possible. She came across a number of claims on the internet about people profiting handsomely from short-term investments. She thot about following them, but ultimately chose to learn first. She paid attention to her current responsibilities, established an emergency fund, and researched fundamental investment principles. When she finally started investing, she only used funds meant for long-term objectives. Her investments lost value a few months later. Anna stuck to her original plan and kept learning instead of selling in a panic. She recognized that the long-term goal of her investment was distinct from short-term market fluctuations. Her failure to forecast the market was her greatest accomplishment. It involved cultivating the self-control to adhere to a methodical approach.

Considering investing as planting a tree is a helpful metaphor. You prepare the soil, select a suitable seed, give the tree the right care, and allow it to grow. It cannot be made to mature overnight. Additionally, you have no control over all weather conditions. Investing is comparable. You manage risk, allocate resources, select suitable assets, and give the strategy time. Strong growth may occur during some times, while declines may occur during others. Although the investor has no control over the market, they do have control over behavior, contributions, diversification, and preparation.

The Smart Growth Path is a straightforward framework that can offer a quick procedure. First, lay the groundwork by ensuring that necessary costs are controllable and that suitable emergency savings are being accumulated. Second, establish your purpose by determining the objective, budget, and time frame for the funds. Third, familiarize yourself with the investment before making a purchase by learning about its features, costs, risks, and possible returns. Fourth, avoid relying solely on one investment by diversifying appropriately. Fifth, make regular contributions that are appropriate for your financial situation. Sixth, review on a regular basis without letting typical market swings dictate every choice.

Because investment funds shouldn't take the place of emergency resources, preparation is crucial. A market downturn may put undue strain on someone who invests money required for rent, food, transportation, or other urgent expenses. An investor can be more patient by keeping short-term needs and long-term investment funds apart. Maintaining long-term investments can be made simpler with a solid financial foundation.

Every investment decision has a purpose when it is defined. Different timelines may be needed for retirement, education, home ownership, business development, and long-term financial independence. Money for an immediate need might require more stability and accessibility than money for a long-term objective. Determining the appropriate level of investment uncertainty requires an understanding of the time horizon.

Acquiring knowledge prior to investing guards against rash decisions. Know what you are purchasing, how it might generate profits, what might result in losses, what fees might be involved, and how simple it is to turn the investment back into cash. Don't make an investment just because a friend, influencer, advertisement, or online community says it will increase. In order to invest responsibly, one must acknowledge the existence of uncertainty.

Another useful defense is diversification. Your financial future may become significantly reliant on a single result if all of your investment funds are concentrated in a single business, sector, or asset. Although diversification can lessen the impact of a bad outcome in one area, it cannot completely eliminate investment risk. Personal circumstances, objectives, and risk tolerance all influence the best course of action.

Often, consistency is more beneficial than attempting to forecast the ideal time to make an investment. Markets are subject to fluctuations, and trying to predict each one can lead to emotional outbursts. Establishing discipline can be facilitated by an inexpensive recurring contribution. Contributions may rise in tandem with income. Developing a routine that can endure various market conditions is the aim.

Examining investments does not entail continuously monitoring them. Over-monitoring can incite excitement during sharp increases or fear during declines. Instead, a periodic review can inquire about whether the investment still aligns with the initial objective, whether the risk level is still appropriate, whether fees are still reasonable, and whether personal circumstances have changed. Attention without obsession is necessary for successful investing.

Understanding that higher potential returns typically entail greater uncertainty is another aspect of smart investing. There isn't a trustworthy way to get big returns without taking any significant risks. It is advisable to exercise caution when dealing with promises of guaranteed profits, urgent opportunities, covert tactics, or exceptionally high returns. Building wealth is typically a gradual process. Tho it can be more in line with long-term financial planning, sustainable progress frequently seems less dramatic than speculative opportunities.

Investing should be used in conjunction with debt management, income generation, saving, and financial security. It shouldn't turn into a stand-alone activity. Contributions to investments may rise if income rises. Priorities might need to be changed if significant debt arises. Financial objectives may shift if family responsibilities do. A flexible approach to investing should be in line with the overall financial picture.

These concepts can be put into practice right away with the help of reflection questions. Which long-term objective would you most like to fund? Do you have enough money to invest without using it for necessities? What level of investment uncertainty would you be willing to put up with before making an emotional choice? Before making a financial commitment, which investment concept do you need to grasp more thoroughly? What practical steps can you take this month to start creating a long-term, reliable investing habit?

It is not necessary to know precisely what the future holds in order to start building wealth. It necessitates planning for various scenarios and adhering to a sensible procedure. Financial stability should come first. Establish your objectives. Prior to acting, learn. Make the right kind of diversification. Make regular contributions. Review on a regular basis. Make your long-term goals clear.

A big starting balance might not be the biggest benefit available to a young adult. Maybe it's time. Time offers a chance for consistent contributions and possible investment growth to cooperate. The longer responsible behaviors can have an impact on financial results, the earlier they are formed.

Don't base your investing success solely on the events of this month or this year. You can gauge it by looking at your level of knowledge, discipline, consistency, and financial readiness. The markets will shift. Your earnings will fluctuate. Your objectives might shift. Throughout all of those changes, your capacity for deliberate decision-making can continue to grow.

Investing is not a quick way to become wealthy. Giving suitable financial resources the chance to support future objectives is a long-term practice. Start cautiously, be realistic about risk, keep learning, and refrain from making decisions motivated by excitement or fear. Maintaining small, regular actions over a long period of time can make them meaningful.

The quality of the decisions you make along the way will have an impact on the wealth you accumulate in the future, in addition to the amount you invest. Get ready before making an investment. Before you commit, make sure you understand. Once you start, maintain consistency. Examine without getting too worked up. When things actually change, make adjustments.

It's not necessary for your initial investment to be substantial. It signifies the start of a habit and the choice to give some of today's resources a purpose that extends beyond today. That habit can contribute to a better financial future with perseverance, self-control, education, and prudent risk management. Building wealth starts when you take deliberate actions that you can sustain over time rather than waiting for the ideal opportunity.

CHAPTER VII

Protecting Financial Progress

Understanding Financial Risk

Since every financial decision contains some degree of uncertainty, understanding financial risk is crucial to developing financial confidence and responsibility. Financial risk is the probability that a choice could lead to financial hardship, losing money, earning less than anticipated, or being unable to fulfill future commitments. A young adult can avoid many avoidable mistakes by learning to identify and manage risk. Although risk cannot be totally eliminated from financial life, it may be recognized, quantified, minimized, and controlled. Avoiding every uncertain scenario is not the aim. Rather, the objective is to make choices that permit probable gains while limiting potential losses to a manageable level.

The fact that different persons experience varying degrees of risk is one of the most crucial concepts regarding financial risk. A choice that makes sense for one individual could be risky for another. How much risk a person may properly accept depends on a number of factors, including income, savings, debt, financial obligations, job security, age, and future objectives. When it comes to handling financial volatility, a person with a steady salary, emergency funds, no debt, and many years till retirement may have more flexibility. A person with substantial debt, minimal savings, or erratic income might need to exercise greater caution. Therefore, understanding one's own situation is a crucial first step before making significant financial decisions.

One of the most well-known types of financial risk is investment risk. Investments may experience a temporary or permanent decline in value. There are many degrees and kinds of risk associated with stocks, bonds, funds, real estate, and other assets. Even if an investment has historically yielded high returns, this does not ensure that it will do so in the future. Economic trends, interest rates, business performance, political changes, consumer behavior, and numerous other factors can all affect market conditions. Young adults should be aware that there is typically more uncertainty associated with bigger potential returns. An investor should think about whether the potential loss is acceptable rather than believing that the investment with the largest potential return is always the best option.

Investment risk can be reduced via diversification. Spreading investments across a variety of assets helps lessen reliance on a single source of performance as opposed to investing all available funds in a single business or asset class. If one investment does poorly, the portfolio may be balanced if another investment does well. Diversification does not ensure that losses won't happen. Numerous investments may lose value concurrently with a general market drop. Diversification, however, can lessen the effects of issues that plague a specific business, sector, or type of investment. As such, it is a crucial long-term risk management tactic.

Another financial risk that young individuals need to be aware of is inflation. When the average cost of goods and services rises over time, money loses purchasing power. This is known as inflation. Because the quantity of money does not change much, it may seem prudent to keep all long-term savings in a low-earning account. That savings, however, might not buy as much in the future if prices increase more quickly than money. This proves that maintaining financial security involves more than just preventing obvious losses. Allowing money to grow too slowly to keep up with growing expenses also carries a danger. Money protection and its ability to retain purchasing power are both taken into account in a balanced financial strategy.

Another significant type of financial risk is created by debt. A person can use borrowing money to manage short-term financial requirements, start a business, finance schooling, or buy necessities. Debt, however, results in liabilities down the road. Missed payments can result in more costs and harm to creditworthiness, and interest charges can raise the total amount owed. Future options may be constrained by taking on more debt than one can afford. A young adult who is aware of the risk associated with debt takes into account not only whether a purchase can be made now but also whether the ensuing payments can be managed in the coming months and years.

Risk related to employment and income should also be taken into account. Financial vulnerability may result from relying solely on one source of income in the event of a job loss, a reduction in working hours, or an unforeseen change that impacts wages. Financial resilience can be strengthened by gaining useful skills, keeping up professional connections, and progressively looking into other sources of income. This does not imply that everyone needs to run several enterprises or have multiple sources of income. It entails being aware that income fluctuates and being ready for that. One of the easiest methods to lessen the financial impact of an unforeseen disruption in income is to create an emergency savings fund.

Since unforeseen costs cannot be avoided, emergency funds are particularly crucial. A household appliance can break down, a car might need repairs, a family obligation might come up, or a significant bill might show up out of the blue. If someone doesn't have any money, they could have to use credit cards or loans to get by. An emergency fund offers a safety net that can lessen the need for costly borrowing. Gradually increasing this reserve can boost confidence and prevent investment funds from being taken out if an unforeseen need arises.

Another option for controlling financial risk is insurance. Some losses may be too big for a person to cover with their own savings comfortably. Insurance can assist in guarding against risks related to health, property, transportation, disability, or other significant financial occurrences, depending on the situation. Eliminating all expense or inconvenience is not always the goal of insurance. Rather, in accordance with the provisions of the policy, it transfers some significant risks to an insurer in return for payments and coverage. Before depending on any insurance policy for safety, it is crucial to understand what is covered, what is not, and what expenses must be met on an individual basis.

Financial danger can also result from emotional decision-making. Financial decisions can be influenced by fear, enthusiasm, impatience, greed, and social pressure. A person might invest in an item because it is popular online, spend more because friends are spending, or sell an investment during a brief fall out of fear. These choices may result in losses that could have been prevented with a well-thought-out plan. A crucial defense against emotional errors can be established by learning to think things through before making big financial decisions. Making more deliberate decisions can result from comparing options, verifying trustworthy information, and taking long-term effects into account.

Another risk that needs to be considered is financial scams. Offers that promise large profits, urgent investment opportunities, covert tactics, or requests to pay money before obtaining comprehensive information should be avoided by young adults. Fraudsters frequently employ emotional appeals and coercion to get people to make snap decisions. A responsible strategy is to independently confirm information, comprehend the precise destination of funds, and refrain from participating in unexplainable ventures. An essential financial talent is the ability to decline opportunities that seem dubious.

Comprehending financial risk does not entail developing a phobia of money or avoiding taking any risks. Calculated risks are often necessary for progress. Investing, business, job advancement, and education can all involve uncertainty while also presenting chances for growth. Preparation is what distinguishes reasonable risk from irresponsible risk. A responsible individual weighs the prospective gains, calculates the potential costs, looks at other options, and assesses if the outcomes can be controlled. With this strategy, one can take advantage of chances without putting the entire financial basis at needless risk.

Understanding financial risk ultimately comes down to developing resilience and making wise decisions. Predicting every event in the future is not necessary for a prosperous financial existence. It relies on anticipating unforeseen events and building sufficient flexibility to adapt to changing conditions. A young adult can lessen needless exposure to major financial issues by keeping emergency reserves, carefully managing debt, diversifying investments, safeguarding valuable assets, honing earning abilities, avoiding emotional decisions, and investigating financial prospects. Although risk will always exist in the world of finance, it need not dictate financial choices. Uncertainty can be faced with confidence, patience, and preparedness rather than dread when risk is recognized and intentionally controlled.

Using Insurance

Building financial security requires using insurance because it helps shield funds, assets, income, and future objectives from unforeseen circumstances. Because they may feel independent, healthy, and unlikely to face significant financial difficulties, young adults may consider insurance to be an unnecessary expense. Unexpected things, however, can occur at any point in life. Expenses that are challenging to handle without protection can result from accidents, property damage, illness, lost income, or damage to valuables. Although insurance cannot stop these occurrences, it can lessen their financial effects and aid in recovery without wiping out years' worth of savings and financial advancements.

Transferring specific financial risks from an individual to an insurance company in exchange for a premium is the fundamental function of insurance. The insurer offers coverage for specific risks under the terms of the policy, and the policyholder pays a predetermined amount in accordance with a predetermined schedule. The insurer may offer financial support in accordance with the terms, limitations, deductibles, and exclusions of the policy if a covered event takes place. Young adults are better able to understand that insurance is more than just another bill when they grasp this fundamental arrangement. It is a financial instrument intended to guard against losses that might be hard or impossible for an individual to bear.

Health coverage is one of the first things young adults should think about. When someone requires emergency care, hospitalization, surgery, medication, or ongoing care, medical costs can add up. Even someone who doesn't often get sick can encounter an unforeseen medical circumstance. A significant medical expense could deplete emergency funds, disrupt investment plans, or result in debt if proper coverage is lacking. When a person needs covered medical services, health insurance can help lower the amount they have to pay out-of-pocket. Before depending on the coverage, it is crucial to comprehend the precise terms because different policies have different benefits, limits, exclusions, deductibles, and payment obligations.

When someone is financially dependent on others, life insurance may also become important. Compared to someone who supports a spouse, children, parents, or other family members, a young adult without dependents might not have as urgent a need for significant life insurance. However, when people start families, buy homes, assume joint financial responsibilities, or take on long-term obligations, their circumstances may change. After the policyholder passes away, life insurance can help designated beneficiaries manage their expenses and financial obligations. The key idea is that insurance needs shouldn't be set in stone; rather, they should adapt to changing obligations.

Other crucial types of financial security include auto and property insurance. A car can be a big financial commitment, and collisions can lead to medical bills, repair costs, legal obligations, or property damage. Having the right auto insurance can help shield against specific liabilities and losses. In a similar vein, homeowners or renters may have priceless possessions that would be costly to replace following theft, fire, specific kinds of damage, or other covered incidents. Instead of presuming that every potential loss is automatically covered, young adults should be aware of what their policies actually cover. Unpleasant surprises can be avoided by being aware of the policy's limitations and exclusions prior to an emergency.

Liability protection is another crucial idea. Sometimes someone can unintentionally hurt someone else or damage someone else's property. The cost of replacing one's own possessions may be far less than the ensuing financial obligation. Certain covered claims may be protected by liability coverage, subject to the terms and limitations of the policy. This demonstrates why property protection should not be the exclusive focus of insurance planning. The financial effects of decisions that could have an impact on other people should also be taken into account.

Comparing coverage is more important when choosing insurance than just picking the lowest premium. Although a low premium might seem appealing, it could have exclusions, lower coverage limits, or higher deductibles that reduce the policy's value in the event of a serious incident. However, paying for excessive coverage can unnecessarily cut into the amount of money available for investments, debt repayment, and savings. A careful strategy takes into account the financial risk, the possible magnitude of the loss, individual circumstances, available resources, and the degree of risk that can be managed without insurance.

It's especially crucial to comprehend deductibles. The amount the policyholder may have to pay before the insurer starts paying for specific qualified expenses is known as the deductible. While a policy with a higher deductible might have lower premiums, one with a lower deductible might need higher premiums. Neither option is inherently superior. Whether a person has enough savings to cover the deductible in the event of a covered event determines the appropriate balance. For this reason, insurance and emergency savings are complementary. While emergency savings can help cover smaller unforeseen expenses and deductibles, insurance may offer protection against significant losses.

Another wise financial practice is to carefully read the policy. Individuals should be aware of what is covered, what is not, how to file a claim, what paperwork might be needed, how deductibles operate, and what coverage limits are in effect. Just because the policy seems complicated doesn't mean that important details should be disregarded. Asking the insurance company or a trained expert for clarification if something is unclear can help avoid misunderstandings. Because the policy seems to offer protection in general, one should never assume that a specific event is covered.

Every time significant financial circumstances change, insurance should also be reviewed. Insurance requirements may change if you start a new job, buy a car, move into a new house, get married, have kids, take on family responsibilities, launch a business, or see a big change in your income. Policies that were suitable a few years ago might not offer enough protection now. Regular evaluations help guaranty that coverage stays in line with present obligations and budgetary objectives. This does not entail buying every kind of insurance that is offered. It entails recognizing significant risks and carefully addressing them.

Because protecting current assets is just as important as increasing them, insurance can also help with long-term wealth building. Consider a young adult who invests and saves for years but is not adequately protected against a significant financial loss. One significant incident might compel that person to sell assets, take out large loans, withdraw investments, or give up on significant financial objectives. The likelihood that one unforeseen incident will undo years of progress can be decreased with the right insurance. In this sense, insurance is no longer just an expense but also a component of wealth preservation.

However, insurance shouldn't take the place of prudent financial management. Long-term investing, responsible debt management, prudent spending practices, and emergency savings are still necessary. The most effective way to use insurance is in conjunction with these other financial strategies. While insurance offers protection against particular risks in accordance with the terms of a policy, savings offer readily available funds for urgent needs. While insurance helps safeguard financial stability in the event of certain unforeseen circumstances, investments are meant to increase wealth over time. A young adult can design a more balanced financial system by comprehending the various functions of these tools.

Developing the practice of prudent insurance use entails being conscious of risk without developing a fear of every potential issue. The objective is not to insure every conceivable scenario. Rather, the objective is to identify potentially catastrophic losses and assess if insurance is a suitable means of handling them. While large risks that could jeopardize financial stability might need more protection, small risks that can be easily managed with savings might not. Instead of encouraging impulsive purchases, this strategy promotes sensible decision-making.

Effective insurance use ultimately comes down to safeguarding the advancements that result from earning, saving, investing, and making prudent financial choices. A solid financial plan acknowledges that unforeseen circumstances can have an impact on wealth in addition to decisions about investments and spending. One method of preparing for those risks is thru insurance. Young adults can make insurance a valuable component of their financial strategy by learning how various policies operate, carefully comparing coverage, comprehending deductibles and exclusions, reviewing protection as circumstances change, and selecting coverage based on actual financial needs. As a result, there is increased resilience, better protection for significant assets and obligations, and a higher likelihood of achieving long-term financial objectives even in the face of unforeseen difficulties.

Building Financial Resilience

Developing the capacity to maintain financial stability in the face of unforeseen difficulties, changes, or obstacles is known as building financial resilience. Financial life is rarely entirely predictable. The cost of daily essentials can be impacted by economic situations, income can fluctuate, expenses can rise, employment can become insecure, and emergencies can strike without warning. Financial resilience gives young adults a foundation that makes it simpler to deal with these circumstances without letting one unforeseen incident ruin years of financial advancement. It goes beyond just possessing a lot of money. Strong habits, adaptability, emergency preparation, responsible debt management, and deliberate decision-making that safeguards future financial stability are all important. A resilient individual plans ahead rather than waiting for a catastrophe to arise because they recognize that financial losses are possible.

Having emergency funds is one of the most crucial pillars of financial resiliency. Money from an emergency fund can be utilized for unforeseen costs without having to rely on credit cards, loans, or other debt right away. A person with no financial funds may be severely strained by an unexpected medical bill, an urgent home repair, a transportation issue, a brief loss of income, or a family obligation. Because it establishes a financial buffer between an unforeseen circumstance and a significant financial setback, even a little emergency fund can offer helpful protection. The essential idea is to start saving regularly, but the exact amount required will depend on individual circumstances, income stability, routine expenses, and obligations. Financial instability can be made more manageable by progressively building an emergency reserve.

Another crucial component of resilience is cost management. When circumstances change, a person who consistently spends all of their earnings has little leeway to react. Income can be allocated between savings, personal needs, financial commitments, and necessary costs by creating a realistic spending plan. A spending plan is not meant to make life unduly tight or to take away enjoyment. Rather, it offers control and knowledge. Understanding spending makes it simpler to pinpoint areas where funds might be cut during trying times. When income drops, or an unforeseen need arises, a person who already understands which expenses are necessary and which can wait can react faster.

Another important factor in financial resilience is debt management. Whether or not income stays steady, debt creates future responsibilities that must be fulfilled. Because interest raises the amount needed to repay the initial borrowing, high-interest debt can become very challenging. There may be less money available for emergencies, savings, investments, or significant opportunities when a sizable amount of income is devoted to debt repayment. Understanding the entire cost of debt before taking it on and taking into account whether payments would still be manageable in various situations are key components of responsible borrowing. Because it gradually lowers monthly payments and increases the amount of income that can be allocated to other priorities, paying off expensive debt can improve financial resilience.

Developing dependable earning capacity is another component of a resilient financial plan. Income is a significant component of financial success, but saving and spending habits are also crucial. By acquiring practical skills, gaining experience, pursuing further education, enhancing professional abilities, and being receptive to new chances, young adults can strengthen their resilience. A more robust skill set can improve one's chances of landing a job, making more money, or adjusting to changes in the workplace or sector. Thus, career development ought to be considered a component of financial planning. Because earning capability frequently affects how much a person can save, invest, and recover from financial challenges, investing in knowledge and skills can have long-term rewards.

When it's suitable, having multiple potential sources of income can also offer more flexibility. This does not always entail working many jobs concurrently. It can entail starting a small business, learning how to operate as a freelancer, doing creative work, providing professional services, or any other respectable source of income that can be increased as needed. When the principal source of income becomes less dependable, additional income can help speed up savings, lower debt, or provide support. Pursuing extra money should, however, be balanced with time, effort, and personal obligations. Working nonstop does not build financial resiliency. It is produced by developing long-lasting methods that boost financial flexibility without posing new challenges.

It is equally crucial to safeguard significant financial resources. Certain risks that could otherwise result in very high costs can be managed with the aid of insurance. Appropriate insurance may offer protection for one's health, property, income, transportation, or other important resources, depending on personal circumstances. The goal is to lessen the financial effect of situations that would be challenging to manage with just personal savings. Because having insurance does not guarantee that every potential expense will be covered, it is crucial to understand coverage, limitations, deductibles, exclusions, and costs. Understanding the safeguards that are currently in place and recognizing important threats that can call for extra protection are key components of sound financial resilience.

Maintaining flexibility is another crucial component. Having options increases a person's financial resiliency. Savings, controllable debt, practical skills, reasonably priced living expenses, dependable transportation, solid business ties, and investments suitable for long-term objectives can all be options. When faced with a setback, someone who has multiple financial options might be able to react without resorting to extreme measures. For instance, having savings can enable someone to carefully consider various employment opportunities instead of jumping at the first chance due to urgent financial strain. People who are flexible have more time to make wiser choices.

Financial resilience can also be enhanced by long-term investing, but only after the necessary short-term financial needs have been met. Although their values can fluctuate, investments can offer chances for development and aid in setting goals for the future. Generally speaking, funds required for urgent crises shouldn't be subjected to needless market risk. A person can avoid selling investments at a bad moment just because an unforeseen expense happened by keeping short-term savings and long-term investments separate. The entire financial plan may become more stable as a result of this division, which gives distinct financial goals for various sums of money.

Emotional self-control is equally necessary for financial resiliency. Making bad decisions might result from feelings of fear, humiliation, annoyance, or pressure brought on by financial difficulties. A person going through a setback could be tempted to make hazardous judgments, sell investments in a panic, ignore debts, or borrow excessively in an effort to bounce back quickly. A resilient person learns to take their time, assess the circumstances, and concentrate on workable alternatives. Financial failures ought to be viewed as issues that need to be resolved rather than as proof of one's own shortcomings. A challenging event can be transformed into a useful financial lesson by reviewing what transpired, determining the cause, and modifying future behavior.

Resilience can be further strengthened by preparing for various scenarios. A young adult can think about what would happen if income temporarily dropped, housing costs rose, transportation got more costly, or an unforeseen requirement emerged rather than assuming that income and spending will always be the same. By considering these scenarios, a financial plan's flaws can be identified before they become significant issues. Perfect future prediction is not necessary for this kind of preparedness. It just entails accepting that change is inevitable and having sufficient adaptability to react to it.

Consistent practices also contribute to the development of financial resilience. Regular small-scale savings can be more sustainable than sporadic large-scale savings. Periodically reviewing spending can help keep wasteful spending from becoming a persistent problem. Timely debt repayment helps safeguard financial advancement. Making better decisions can be achieved by learning about financial products. Even though each of these acts can seem insignificant on its own, over time, their impacts can mount up. Strong financial resilience is typically developed by consistent, everyday choices rather than a single, spectacular financial success.

Developing a financial life that can endure hardship without losing focus is ultimately what it means to have financial resilience. Although setbacks and emergencies cannot always be avoided, their consequences can frequently be lessened by being prepared. Appropriate insurance can transfer some significant risks, career development can increase earning power, emergency savings can offer immediate protection, good debt management can lower commitments, and careful investing can promote long-term growth. However, emotional control and adaptable planning can help someone react coolly as things shift. These behaviors provide a young adult with more than just financial stability. Because the individual is aware that unforeseen difficulties do not always equate to financial collapse, they foster self-assurance and independence. Even when things don't go exactly as planned, resilience enables setbacks to become transient rather than permanent hurdles, allowing one to keep working toward important goals.

Creating Your Financial Safety Shield

Building wealth is only one aspect of achieving financial security, so safeguarding financial advancement is important. Making sure that the advancements you have already made can withstand unforeseen difficulties is the other aspect. A single significant setback can undermine years of progress if there is no safeguard in place, even though income, savings, investments, and debts can all rise and fall. Pressure can be quickly created by an emergency, a loss of income, an unforeseen family obligation, a significant repair, financial fraud, or a bad choice. Not every issue can be avoided with a financial safety net. Rather, it gets you ready to react without undermining the foundation you've worked so hard to build.

By putting this idea into practice, your perspective on financial success is altered. Rather than gauging your progress solely by your income or accumulation, you start thinking about how resilient you are. When it comes to emergency savings, insurance, account security, responsible borrowing, financial records, and risk management, you become more deliberate. Because your money is not just being accumulated, this strengthens your financial position. It is safeguarded. When you incorporate protection into your daily financial routine, unforeseen circumstances become manageable challenges rather than catastrophes that inevitably derail your plans.

Ignoring financial security can have detrimental effects. A person may be forced to sell investments during a bad time even though their investment account is growing and they have no emergency savings. A person with a high income might have a lot of debt and find that losing their job makes it impossible to pay their bills each month. Someone else might neglect to safeguard financial accounts, leaving them open to fraud. These circumstances show why accumulation is not the only way to think about wealth. Maintaining progress is equally crucial.

Increased confidence is the practical effect of financial protection. You can make decisions with less fear when you are aware that you have emergency resources and systems built to lower significant risks. Because you are not entirely reliant on your next pay check, you might have more freedom to start a business, pursue education, change jobs, or take care of your family. Breathing room is created by financial protection. Instead of responding quickly to pressure, it allows you to think things through.

By the end of this chapter, you will be able to recognize the financial risks that could impede your progress, develop workable safeguards to protect your financial information and income, savings, and assets, and set up a routine review system to ensure that your protection plan remains appropriate as your circumstances change. These skills make financial protection an active practice instead of something that is only taken into consideration after a crisis arises.

A young employee who has accumulated several months' worth of savings and begun investing for long-term objectives is a concrete example. The employee distinguishes between investment funds and emergency savings rather than considering the entire amount as available money. While long-term investments are given time to grow, the emergency fund is meant for actual unforeseen needs. Additionally, the employee reviews available financial protection, employs robust account security, and maintains the organization of crucial financial documents. The emergency savings can help pay for an unforeseen medical or household expense without requiring the employee to sell long-term investments or heavily rely on costly borrowing.

A brief narrative highlights the value of planning. Daniel, a young employee, had been saving money and paying off debt for a number of years. He thot he was finally secure financially. Then, for a few months, his employer cut back on his working hours. Daniel was able to use a portion of his savings while searching for extra income because he had already established an emergency fund and kept his monthly obligations reasonable. Although uncomfortable, the circumstance did not impede his financial advancement. If someone had no savings and faced the same reduction, they might have taken out a loan or sold valuable assets right away. The setback was not avoided by Daniel's preparation. It kept the setback from turning into a financial catastrophe.

Financial protection can be compared to a safety net surrounding a developing structure, which is a helpful metaphor. Imagine constructing a home and then abandoning it to extreme weather. Even though the structure is sturdy, damage could result from frequent storms if it is not protected. Your assets, income, investments, and savings are similar to the structure. The shield surrounding them is made up of emergency funds, suitable security, safe accounts, controllable debt, and meticulous preparation. Not every storm is prevented by the shield. It lessens the damage and increases the likelihood that the structure will continue to be strong.

The Financial Safety Shield is a straightforward framework that can be put to use right away. First, determine which risks could have a major impact on your financial situation. Second, set aside a sufficient amount of accessible savings to cover suitable unforeseen costs. Third, use appropriate safeguards to protect income and valuable assets. Fourth, protect your accounts and financial data. Fifth, limit needless exposure by managing high debt and hazardous financial choices. Sixth, periodically review your protection and make any necessary updates.

Finding vulnerabilities is the first step. Imagine what would happen if your income abruptly dropped, a necessary expense surfaced, your personal data was compromised, or a significant obligation arose. You don't have to envision every potential catastrophe. Concentrate on actual occurrences that might result in significant financial harm. Knowing your biggest weaknesses enables you to focus on the areas where protection is most important.

One of the easiest preventative measures is to create easily accessible emergency savings. Income, expenses, job security, obligations, and individual circumstances all influence the amount needed. Establishing a reserve that can be utilized for true emergencies rather than regular expenses is what counts. A small reserve can be a useful first line of defense. The reserve can be reviewed and modified as income and responsibilities rise.

Another aspect of the shield is the protection of income and valuable assets. Appropriate insurance or other financial protections may help lessen the financial impact of significant events, depending on your situation. Purchasing every type of protection is not the goal. It involves identifying the risks that could have serious financial repercussions and figuring out which risks can be transferred, minimized, or controlled with the resources at hand.

Safeguarding accounts and personal data is also essential for financial security. Create strong, one-of-a-kind passwords, activate the security features that are available, keep an eye on your financial transactions, and be wary of unsolicited requests for cash or private information. In addition to bad investment choices, avoidable security errors can also hinder financial advancement. Thus, safeguarding your accounts is a component of safeguarding your wealth.

Additionally, debt management makes the safety net stronger. When income fluctuates, large fixed obligations may limit flexibility. It may be simpler to react to unforeseen events if debt is kept under control. Before taking on new debt, think about whether the payment would still be manageable if your income or expenses changed, in addition to whether it is currently affordable.

Keeping financial records is another crucial safeguard. Organize important documents and be aware of the safe locations for accessing crucial account information. Because you can quickly ascertain what resources, obligations, and protections are available, knowing your financial situation makes managing emergencies easier.

These concepts can be put into practice right away with the help of reflection questions. What financial development might have the biggest impact on your present circumstances? How equipped are you to deal with an unforeseen necessary expense without taking out a loan? Which aspect of your financial life is currently least protected? Which financial safety or account security measure should you strengthen this month? When your goals and income responsibilities change, what regular review habit will help you maintain a strong financial safety net?

Anticipating the worst is not the goal of financial protection. It is about acknowledging the unpredictability of everyday life. Although it's impossible to predict when things will change, you can plan for plausible outcomes. You have options when you are prepared. You have flexibility when you have options. You can make wiser choices under duress if you are flexible.

Wealth building is also more sustainable when there is a robust safety net. Your financial progress is more likely to continue when emergencies do not automatically force you to halt long-term investments, take out costly loans, or give up on significant objectives. Thus, growth is aided by protection. It is not appropriate to view the two as conflicting priorities. By safeguarding what you already have, you can build a stronger foundation for future growth.

As your life changes, so should your financial safety net. A person managing substantial assets or providing for a family may require a different level of protection than someone with a first job and few responsibilities. Examine your emergency savings, debt levels, financial security procedures, and other precautions as your income, commitments, and responsibilities change.

Eliminating all financial risks is not the aim. That is not feasible. The objective is to become sufficiently prepared so that years of progress are not automatically destroyed by common setbacks. Create reserves. Control your responsibilities. Safeguard vital resources. Protect your accounts. Examine your weaknesses. Continue your education.

When financial progress can withstand challenging times, it becomes more valuable. Your savings, investments, abilities, and future opportunities can all be safeguarded by the habits you establish today. Prepare your safety shield gradually and keep it up to date. You won't have to start over from scratch when unforeseen difficulties arise. You'll have a more solid base from which to bounce back, carry on constructing, and confidently face the future.

CHAPTER VIII

Growing Long Term Wealth

Understanding Wealth Creation

Understanding that having a high salary is not the same as having wealth is the first step in understanding how wealth is developed. Income, on the other hand, is the money that an individual obtains from employment, business ventures, investments, or other sources. Wealth, on the other hand, refers to the valuable resources that an individual accumulates after taking into account their debts and financial commitments. If an individual spends most of their income immediately or uses it to pay off excessive debt, they may have a high wage but still be in debt. At the same time, a person with a low salary can gradually accumulate significant wealth by controlling their spending, saving money regularly, making prudent investments, reducing unnecessary debt, and building valuable assets.

To increase one's wealth, one of the most important pillars is to create a positive difference between one's income and one's expenses. It is difficult to transform money that has been earned into a source of future financial success if it is wasted immediately after it has been earned. The implication of this is not that one should not take pleasure in life or that every purchase is a mistake. On the contrary, it suggests that spending ought to be done with intentionality. A young adult can examine their regular expenses to determine which are essential, which provide genuine value, and which can be reduced. Whenever a certain amount of money is consistently left over after expenses, it can be put toward investments, debt reduction, savings for unexpected expenses, education, or other beneficial endeavors.

Savings serves as the foundation for both the accumulation of wealth and the maintenance of financial stability. Before risking a significant amount of money on an investment, it is beneficial to set aside funds that can be accessed if unexpected expenses arise. An individual who has emergency savings may be able to avoid having to borrow money on unfavorable terms or sell investments at the wrong time due to a necessary medical expense, an urgent repair, a temporary loss of income, or a family obligation. Another way to create opportunities is to save money. When a significant opportunity presents itself, a person who has money on hand is more flexible and able to respond appropriately. Consequently, developing a habit of saving money consistently is beneficial for both future growth and protection.

Accumulated funds can be used to expand profitable assets through investing. Stocks, bonds, funds, real estate, and other assets are all examples of investments that can be made, depending on the individual's circumstances and their level of comfort with risk. When you invest, you expose yourself to risk, and no single investment will guarantee positive results. It is for this reason that the pursuit of rapid profits or the attempt to forecast short-term changes in the market should not serve as the basis for the accumulation of wealth. One of the components of a more effective strategy is acquiring knowledge about how various assets operate, understanding risk, appropriately diversifying assets, considering expenses, and maintaining a focus on the long term.

If you want to build wealth, time is one of the most important benefits. Profits from investments can generate additional profits in the future if they are carried over into subsequent investments. Over prolonged periods, this compounding process can become more effective. Young people can have more time to make contributions and build up their future investment growth if they start saving and investing at an earlier age. Although the initial investment might not be very large, with enough time and perseverance, consistent contributions can eventually become quite substantial. For this reason, developing good financial habits at a young age can have a significant impact on the financial stability one will experience in the future.

In addition, human capital is an essential component of wealth. A number of factors can contribute to an individual's ability to generate income, including knowledge, education, professional experience, technical skills, communication abilities, and problem-solving skills. It is possible that one of the best financial decisions a young adult can make is to put money into the acquisition of practical skills. When you have a higher earning potential, you have more options for investing, saving, paying down debt, and preparing for future goals. Therefore, rather than being regarded as something that is separate from financial planning, career advancement ought to be regarded as a component of the process of financial wealth creation.

Additionally essential is the management of debt. Because interest payments consume income that could be put toward productive assets, high-cost debt can be detrimental to the accumulation of wealth. An individual's financial freedom may be restricted by needless debt, despite the fact that prudent borrowing can occasionally assist in the accomplishment of beneficial goals. It is possible for a person to make better choices if they are aware of the monthly commitments, interest rates, payback terms, and total costs associated with borrowing money. Repaying expensive debt can contribute to the strengthening of the financial foundation by releasing future income that can be used for investments and savings.

In the end, the process of accumulating wealth is a gradual one that is made up of numerous decisions. This Includes the generation of income, the management of expenditures, the accumulation of savings, the acquisition of useful skills, the management of debt, the protection of assets, and the scheduling of time to work toward long-term goals. It is not the only way to amass wealth to have expensive possessions or a high salary; there are other alternatives as well. The production of wealth occurs when an individual consistently converts a portion of their existing resources into increased financial capability for the future. A young adult can gradually improve their financial situation, become more self-sufficient, and potentially have more options in the future if they establish certain habits at an early age and continue to adhere to them despite the fact that their circumstances are constantly changing.

Building Multiple Assets

Developing a variety of assets is crucial to building long-term financial strength because depending solely on one source of wealth can make one susceptible to unforeseen changes. Resources with a monetary value that could support future growth, security, or income are called assets. Building assets for a young adult does not always entail buying pricey homes or making significant investments right away. The first step is to make it a habit to convert a portion of your current income into resources that will be valuable in the future. A stronger financial foundation can be built over time by combining savings, investments, real estate, business interests, professional skills, and other valuable resources.

Accessible savings are among the first things a young adult can accumulate. Savings offer flexibility and financial stability, but they might not yield the same growth potential as some investments. Without having to sell investments or take on costly debt, an emergency fund can assist in covering unforeseen costs. Planned opportunities like education, career advancement, moving, or launching a small business can also be supported by savings. Establishing this financial reserve is a crucial first step since it offers a starting point for the development of other assets.

Long-term growth can also come from investment assets. A person may think about diversified investments like stocks, bonds, mutual funds, exchange-traded funds, or other suitable assets, depending on their financial situation and risk tolerance. Every investment has unique characteristics, costs, risks, and potential returns. Developing a variety of assets does not entail purchasing every product on the market. It entails assembling resources in a deliberate manner that fulfills various functions. Although it cannot prevent investment losses or ensure profits, diversification can lessen reliance on the performance of a single investment.

For some people, property can also become a valuable asset. A place to live, potential appreciation, rental income, and other financial advantages can all be found in real estate. But owning a property comes with a lot of expenses and obligations, such as upkeep, insurance, taxes, financing, and repairs. Instead of buying just because owning a property seems to indicate financial success, one should think about whether it fits their long-term objectives and financial circumstances. While an excessive financial commitment can limit opportunities and cause stress, an affordable property that supports a person's goals can be helpful.

Owning a business is an additional method of accumulating assets. Customers, reputation, systems, intellectual property, equipment, brand, and profitability are all factors that can make a business valuable. Young adults can start small by freelancing, selling goods, providing services, or building a business around a practical skill. Owning a business entails risk, and success is never assured, but a well-run company can generate revenue as well as an asset that might increase in value over time. Focusing on delivering true value, controlling expenses, comprehending clients, and developing sustainable operations are crucial.

One should also think of human capital as an asset. Future earning potential can be increased by an individual's knowledge, experience, skills, professional connections, and problem-solving abilities. Human capital, in contrast to a physical asset, is developed via practice, education, training, and experience. A young adult may be able to earn more money over the course of their career if they invest in useful skills. By saving and investing, that extra income can then be transformed into financial assets. In this sense, acquiring skills can serve as the foundation for creating a variety of other types of wealth.

Understanding the distinction between productive and nonproductive possessions is also necessary for building multiple assets. Certain purchases might be convenient or enjoyable without producing significant financial value. Spending money on these items is perfectly acceptable, but they should not be confused with assets that increase wealth. Generally speaking, a productive asset has the capacity to produce income, increase in value, lower future expenses, or offer another significant financial advantage. Knowing this difference enables one to assess purchases based on their long-term impact rather than their outward appearance.

Avoiding over-concentration is another key idea. An unforeseen issue in one area can result in significant financial harm if almost all of an individual's wealth is linked to a single employer, business, property, or investment. By distributing resources among various opportunities, building multiple assets can increase resilience. For instance, an individual may have a small business interest, professional skills, diversified investments, and emergency savings. These resources have distinct functions and may react to economic circumstances in different ways. Diversification should always be suitable for each person's situation, objectives, and risk tolerance.

Since significant financial resources typically develop gradually, building multiple assets requires patience. A young adult might start with modest investments and a small savings account. Contributions can be increased as income rises. Over time, those contributions might help fund additional investments, the growth of a business, or the acquisition of real estate. Over many years, consistent financial behavior can produce significant results, even though the process may initially seem slow. Instead of aiming for quick financial success, the emphasis should be on creating a sustainable system.

Building assets and managing income are closely related. A person has the chance to allocate a portion of their increased income toward productive resources when their income rises. Higher income, however, can result in higher living expenses if discipline is lacking. Accelerating asset accumulation can be achieved by increasing savings and investment contributions while maintaining reasonable spending. Eliminating all lifestyle enhancements is not necessary for this. Instead of letting every extra peso be used for new expenses, it entails allowing financial advancement to benefit from increased earning power.

Because liabilities can reduce the value of assets, debt management is just as crucial. A person may have expensive debt that drastically lowers their net financial position in addition to investments and real estate. Thus, it is necessary to consider both aspects of the financial picture when building assets. Eliminating expensive debt can increase net worth and free up future earnings for the purchase of more assets. Borrowing should be carefully considered, particularly if the debt is being used for consumption rather than for a reasonably long-term financial benefit.

Another essential step in the process is asset protection. A person may become vulnerable if they accumulate wealth without taking possible losses into account. Protecting accumulated resources can be aided by appropriate insurance, emergency savings, safe financial accounts, cautious investment diversification, and upkeep of property. The goal of protection is to stop one unforeseen incident from ruining years of advancement, not to eliminate all risks completely.

Making better financial decisions can also be achieved by routinely evaluating assets. Savings, investments, real estate, business ventures, debts, and career advancement can all be reviewed on a regular basis. This analysis can show if resources are still in line with financial objectives. While some assets might no longer be suitable, others might require more care. Frequent reviews also give you the chance to think about whether the overall level of risk has become inappropriate or whether contributions should rise in response to changes in income.

Creating a financial structure that can eventually offer more stability, flexibility, and opportunity is the ultimate goal of building multiple assets. Savings for security, investments for long-term growth, real estate when suitable, business interests, and useful skills that boost earning potential can all contribute to a solid financial foundation. Financial success doesn't have to be solely dependent on one asset. A young adult can build a more resilient financial position by progressively creating various forms of value, managing debt responsibly, safeguarding accumulated resources, and exercising patience. Having more possessions is not the biggest advantage of accumulating multiple assets. A person can become less reliant on a single salary or investment and more equipped to handle shifting opportunities and challenges as a result of having more options and sources of financial strength.

Maintaining Wealth Growth

It takes more than just increasing income and making wise investments to sustain wealth growth. The goal is to design a financial system that can adapt to changing circumstances and yet function well. A young adult can start accumulating wealth by setting aside a percentage of their salary, paying off debt, making regular investments, and learning useful job skills. The next difficulty, nonetheless, is maintaining and expanding what has already been established once these habits start to show benefits. Because lifestyle inflation, emotional spending, bad investment choices, excessive debt, and a lack of preparation for unforeseen circumstances may rapidly undermine financial gains, maintaining wealth needs discipline. The objective is to establish a long-lasting relationship with money rather than to grow fixated on it. Every wise choice made over time leads to increased stability and freedom when wealth building is included in a long-term financial habit.

Consistency is one of the most crucial factors in sustaining wealth growth. Rarely does one exceptional choice determine financial success. It is more frequently the result of repeated, first insignificant actions. While managing spending, avoiding needless borrowing, investing sensibly, and saving on a regular basis may not seem thrilling, they can have significant effects if they are maintained over an extended period of time. A young adult's expenditures shouldn't necessarily rise in tandem with their income. Rather, a portion of each increase in income might be allocated to investments, debt reduction, savings, or other beneficial financial objectives. This strategy enables rapid financial advancement without necessitating significant compromises. Because a person becomes less reliant on ideal circumstances to maintain financial stability, consistency also fosters resilience.

Protecting collected assets is also necessary to sustain wealth growth. A false sense of security can result from accumulating riches without safeguarding them. If there is no financial cushion, a person may be forced to sell investments or take on costly debt due to an unforeseen medical expenditure, job loss, significant repair, family emergency, or a time of reduced income. Thus, an emergency fund is crucial to maintaining long-term prosperity. This reserve's main objective is not to produce financial returns. Its goal is to offer stability in the event of unforeseen costs. A young adult can avoid upsetting an investment plan just because an unexpected expenditure comes up by maintaining emergency funds apart from long-term investments. Appropriate insurance, cautious debt management, safe account habits, and keeping crucial financial records are more examples of financial security.

Controlling lifestyle inflation is another important component of sustaining wealth growth. nicer homes, newer technology, more frequent travel, nicer clothes, or more expensive entertainment are all natural desires as income rises. It's not always unethical to take advantage of increased income. The issue arises when every gain in income is instantly translated into increased ongoing costs. Even with considerably more income, the amount available for investing and saving may remain disappointingly tiny if fixed expenses increase too quickly. Allowing lifestyle enhancements while purposefully allocating a sizeable amount of extra income to wealth accumulation is a viable strategy. This strikes a balance between savoring the moment and safeguarding the future. Increased income improves both the quality of life and the stability of the financial base, making financial independence easier.

Another crucial element is investment management. It is not necessary to continuously buy and sell investments in an effort to maximize return in order to maintain wealth growth. Overdoing it might lead to emotional choices and needless expenses. Alternatively, investors can concentrate on regular evaluation, reasonable time horizons, suitable risk levels, and diversification. Risk should still be recognized rather than disregarded, even if a young adult who has many years before needing to invest money may be able to withstand greater market volatility than someone who is getting close to a significant financial objective. Personal goals, financial capability, and tolerance for short-term losses should all be taken into consideration while making investment decisions. Determining whether investments are still in line with those goals might be aided by regular portfolio assessments. After a period of excellent performance, rebalancing when necessary can also keep one asset category from growing unduly large.

Understanding the distinction between constructive and destructive debt is also necessary to sustain wealth growth. The financial impact of borrowing varies. High interest debt used for needless expenditure may have a different long-term effect than debt supporting education, business development, or another properly considered opportunity. Any borrowing should be assessed based on its cost, intended use, and impact on future cash flow. Young individuals may find it challenging to continue saving and investing if they let debt payments take up a significant amount of their income. Because money that would otherwise be spent on interest can be diverted into wealth-producing endeavors, keeping debt reasonable safeguards future revenue. Maintaining financial momentum can therefore be greatly aided by keeping an eye on interest rates, repayment plans, and total borrowing costs.

The plan for maintaining wealth should continue to include income growth. Although one cannot always control market returns, there are frequently chances to increase one's earning potential. Future earning potential can be increased by developing professional abilities, going to school, getting experience, enhancing communication, establishing a solid reputation, and comprehending shifting demands in the workplace. Increased income generates more funds for investments and savings. The true benefit, though, arises when higher income is paired with sound financial management. Increasing income without practicing sound money management could result in increased expenditure. The amount available for long-term wealth growth can be greatly increased by increasing earnings while keeping spending under control.

Treating money as a system rather than a collection of discrete choices is a helpful way to think about sustaining wealth growth. Income enters the system, expenses are controlled, savings offer security, investments seek expansion, insurance helps transfer certain risks, and debt is managed to prevent future cash flow from becoming overwhelmed. Every component affects the others. Investing may decrease if expenditure increases significantly. Interest payments may deplete savings if debt gets costly. Investments may need to be sold at a bad time if emergency savings are insufficient. Financial progress is more stable when these components work together. The goal is balance and consistent correction, not perfection.

Patience is also necessary for long-term wealth maintenance. Financial objectives might change, occupations can shift, and markets can rise and fall. When investments momentarily fall or when growth appears to be slower than anticipated, a young adult may become disheartened. However, a long-term strategy does not always fail because of short-term failures. People may sell investments during uncertain times or make hasty financial judgments due to emotional reactions. Gaining patience enables one to consider situations carefully rather than reacting instinctively. This does not imply that real financial issues should be disregarded. It entails differentiating between circumstances that call for a fundamental shift and transient alterations.

Maintaining this equilibrium might be aided by routine financial evaluations. Income, expenses, savings, investments, debt, insurance coverage, and key goal progress can all be reviewed on a regular basis. The goal is to determine what is effective and what requires improvement. A financial plan is not something that should be made once and then forgotten. It ought to change as conditions do. Adjustments may be necessary due to a new job, marriage, home purchase, business opportunity, family responsibilities, or significant change in income. Frequent evaluations facilitate early detection of these changes and intentional response.

In the end, sustaining wealth expansion entails safeguarding the behaviors that initially led to financial advancement while consistently enhancing the system. It is not appropriate to view wealth as something that may be accumulated and then neglected. It calls for awareness, self-control, tolerance, and adaptability. Time is the biggest benefit for a young adult. While sound financial practices can become firmly ingrained, money that is saved and invested appropriately may benefit from extended periods of growth. A person can build a financial foundation capable of sustaining future chances by limiting lifestyle inflation, safeguarding against emergencies, carefully managing debt, boosting earning capacity, evaluating investments, and continuously allocating resources toward worthwhile goals. Reaching a particular financial goal is not the most valuable accomplishment. It involves acquiring the skills and routines required to maintain financial advancement in the face of shifting conditions. Each stage of life can build upon the one before it when wealth is intentionally maintained, resulting in increased stability, adaptability, and confidence for the future.

Strengthening Your Wealth Foundation

When financial knowledge is applied consistently, long-term wealth takes on significance. It is helpful to understand how wealth can increase, but knowledge by itself cannot alter a person's financial future. When you make conscious choices about how much money you keep, where you put it, how you safeguard it, and how consistently you let it grow, that's when the real change starts. Early adoption of these habits by a young adult increases the likelihood that future income will turn into valuable capital. By making decisions that can be repeated over many years, that person starts to create financial stability rather than relying solely on future raises, unforeseen opportunities, or good fortune.

You can gradually alter your perspective on money by putting these ideas into practice. A more expensive lifestyle is no longer a prerequisite for a higher income. Extra cash can be used to boost savings, ease financial strain, buy useful assets, or make investments for long-term objectives. Due to their connection to a broader financial direction, small decisions start to become more significant. Neglecting these behaviors can have the opposite effect. Because spending increases at the same rate as income, financial security may not improve. Because available funds are frequently spent rather than allocated toward future value, years may go by without significant advancement. Therefore, the real-world impact of wealth building comes from making a difference between your income and expenses and then making deliberate use of that difference.

By the end of this chapter, you will be able to choose financial actions that promote future growth rather than immediate consumption, identify realistic ways to convert a portion of your income into long-term assets, and develop a consistent habit of evaluating and enhancing your financial progress. These skills can assist you in transitioning from merely making money to consciously accumulating financial assets. They can also assist you in realizing that wealth is the result of numerous wise choices made over time rather than a single, dramatic financial decision.

Imagine a young employee with a modest monthly salary who gets a slight pay raise. The employee chooses to split the extra money rather than buying a new phone right away, going out to eat more often, and spending more on entertainment. A portion is allocated to a long-term investment account, a portion to an emergency fund, and a smaller portion is available for enjoyment. The individual does not let the entire increase vanish into lifestyle expenses, but they still reap the benefits of having a higher income. After a number of years, the person has accumulated investments and savings that were previously non-existent. The precise amount saved is not the key lesson. The choice to give increased income a purpose before letting increased spending absorb it is the lesson.

This idea is demonstrated by a short story. Consider Daniel and Marco, two young friends who start working at roughly the same age. They both want to enjoy their independence and have comparable salaries. Every time his income rises, Daniel progressively increases his spending. He travels frequently, purchases more expensive things, and uses credit when his savings aren't enough. Marco takes pleasure in his earnings as well, but he first safeguards a portion of each rise. He accumulates savings, makes regular investments, and becomes knowledgeable about assets that may increase in value over time. Even though Daniel's income has increased over the past ten years, he still feels under financial strain because a large portion of it goes toward sustaining his way of life. Although Marco doesn't appear to be significantly wealthier from the outside, he has amassed financial resources that provide him with options. One lucky investment was not the source of the difference. It was the result of repeated actions.

Considering wealth as a tree is a helpful metaphor. Assets are the roots and branches that enable the tree to grow stronger and eventually produce something valuable, whereas income is like the water that reaches the tree. The tree has little chance of growing if all the water is drained away right away. Over time, the tree can become more stable if some of the available resources are continuously used to strengthen the roots. Similarly, money that is regularly spent yields short-term satisfaction, but money that is purposefully allocated to investments, savings, useful assets, and productive skills can lead to increased stability in the future. The intention is not to cease having fun. Making sure that some of today's resources contribute to tomorrow's strength is the aim.

The Grow and Protect Method is a straightforward framework that can make this feasible. Start by calculating the amount that consistently remains after necessary expenses based on your current income. Next, safeguard your financial base by keeping an emergency fund that is suitable for your situation. Next, allocate a steady percentage of your available funds to long-term investments or assets that align with your objectives and risk tolerance. Then, enhance your financial capability by acquiring useful skills, looking for better opportunities, or creating new revenue streams. Lastly, evaluate your progress on a regular basis and modify your plan if your circumstances, goals, income, or responsibilities change.

Measuring your starting position honestly is the first step. Put your income, essential spending, current savings, debts, investments, and significant financial commitments in writing. While doing this, don't be critical of yourself. Optimistic assumptions are less helpful than accurate information. Finding your financial gap—the amount that could be put toward future objectives after necessary expenditures—is the second step. Giving that sum a purpose is the third step. While some might be prepared to increase long-term investments or pursue profitable opportunities, others might need to strengthen their savings first. To ensure that progress is not solely dependent on motivation, the fourth step is to automate what can be automated. Rather than waiting for a significant financial issue, the fifth step is to review the system and make minor adjustments regularly.

For instance, a person with five hundred units of extra money each month might choose to invest some of it for long-term objectives, save some of it until a suitable emergency fund is created, and use the rest for personal priorities. Depending on income, expenses, debt, obligations, and risk tolerance, the precise distribution will vary. The decision's intentionality is what counts. When a financial system can function during regular months instead of needing ideal circumstances, it becomes powerful.

Recognizing lifestyle inflation is one of the most significant applications. It is normal to desire better food, entertainment, clothes, technology, or more comfortable living conditions when one's income rises. It is not intrinsically bad to appreciate advancements. Every increase in income turns into an increase in ongoing expenses, which is dangerous. Reducing spending can be challenging once it becomes the norm. Allowing lifestyle improvements while purposefully setting aside a portion of each income increase for future financial growth is a more effective strategy.

Patience is another crucial application. Building wealth seldom yields immediate, dramatic results. Due to the small amounts saved or invested, early progress may appear insignificant. On the other hand, consistency allows time to work. Early adoption of sound financial practices gives a young adult something very valuable that cannot be bought later in the same manner: time. A person's ability to influence future financial circumstances increases with the age at which they start making disciplined decisions.

Ignoring this procedure may result in unanticipated expenses. A person might put off learning until a financial crisis strikes, saving until a higher salary arrives, investing until all debts are paid off, or planning until retirement seems imminent. Future options may be diminished with each delay. There is never a perfect time to start. An ambitious plan that is shelved after a few months is frequently less valuable than a modest start that can be sustained.

When reflection results in action, it is most beneficial. Consider this: What proportion of my present income is genuinely improving my financial situation in the future? Which spending habit could I cut back on without drastically lowering my standard of living? What skill or financial asset could I start consistently honing this year? If I kept up my current habits, how would my financial situation look in five years? What specific financial step can I take this week to make my foundation stronger?

Gaining more money on a statement is not the only goal of wealth building. Financial resources can increase your flexibility, lessen your reliance on debt, open doors, and give you the confidence to handle unforeseen circumstances. Being wealthy can free you from continual financial pressure and enable you to make decisions based on priorities. It can help you support those you love, take advantage of worthwhile opportunities, get ready for old age, and make more independent decisions.

Ordinary actions carried out consistently provide the strongest foundation. Prior to the money running out, save. Invest based on a well-considered plan. Defend yourself from significant setbacks. Continue to increase your earning capacity. Evaluate your progress in an honest manner. Don't let fleeting wants dictate long-term financial choices. Above all, keep in mind that financial advancement does not necessitate excellence. It calls for focus, perseverance, consistency, and a readiness to make corrections.

What you consistently do with the resources at your disposal today will determine your financial future. Every dollar saved, every needless expense avoided, every practical skill acquired, and every well-considered investment can be incorporated into a larger framework. Start with what you can control, develop the habit, fortify the system, and give yourself time to contribute to the outcome. Although the foundation may start out quietly, it can grow strong enough to provide long-term security and increased financial freedom with consistent action.

CHAPTER IX

Planning Your Financial Future

Setting Financial Goals

Establishing financial objectives is crucial to creating a solid and well-organized financial strategy since they provide direction for financial decisions. Without goals, it can be simple to spend money without thinking about what you'll need in the future, put off saving, or make financial decisions based mostly on what you want right now. A financial objective gives a clear justification for investing, saving, lowering debt, or raising income. Setting objectives can help a young adult transform aspirations for financial success into concrete activities that can be tracked and enhanced over time. Building emergency funds, funding schooling, buying a house, launching a business, getting ready for retirement, traveling, helping family members, or becoming financially independent are some examples of goals. Setting goals is meant to give a structure that enables money to support important priorities rather than to put undue pressure on people.

A practical financial objective should be sufficiently detailed to direct activity. It may sound inspiring to state that one wants to become wealthy, but it doesn't outline the necessary actions. What is needed, how much money might be needed, and when the money should be available are all identified in a more helpful aim. For instance, setting aside a specific sum for an emergency fund establishes a more precise goal than merely choosing to increase savings. Setting a clear objective makes it simpler to assess if progress is being made and how much has to be saved on a regular basis. Clear financial goals make it easier to make everyday decisions since spending and saving can be assessed based on whether they contribute to the intended result.

Another crucial component of financial goal-setting is time. In general, there are three types of goals: short-term, medium-term, and long-term. Building up starting savings, paying a bill, paying off a small debt, or buying a significant item are examples of short-term objectives. Savings for a home, a car, a company, or education are examples of medium-term objectives. Retirement, financial freedom, and building enduring wealth are examples of long-term objectives. Every time period calls for a unique strategy. While money meant for long-term objectives may have more time to benefit from long-term investments, money needed shortly may potentially need to stay reasonably accessible and shielded from needless market volatility. Knowing the time horizon makes it easier to make sure that the financial plan aligns with the funds' intended use.

Setting priorities is particularly essential because a young adult may have multiple financial aspirations concurrently. Saving for a trip, investing, buying pricey things, paying off debt, and accumulating emergency funds all at once can be alluring. However, having a limited income frequently necessitates making decisions. Setting priorities does not entail permanently giving up on less significant objectives. It entails deciding which goals should be prioritized. Prioritizing managing costly debt and creating a basic emergency fund may be more important than allocating substantial sums of money to discretionary objectives. Other objectives can be given more focus if the fundamental financial underpinnings are in place. Financial planning should be flexible since priorities might shift as situations do.

Setting a financial objective is just the first step. The objective needs to be linked to a workable plan. The needed monthly or weekly payment should be taken into consideration if a person wants to save a certain amount within a specific time frame. This gives the objective greater substance and shows whether it is now feasible. If the needed amount is too high, the person can raise income, lower the aim, extend the deadline, or modify spending. This procedure is beneficial because it substitutes realistic planning for nebulous optimism. A goal should be both difficult enough to spur advancement and doable enough to keep people from giving up.

Setting financial goals is closely related to budgeting. A budget offers a framework for allocating funds to critical goals. A portion of the money received might be allocated to savings, debt repayment, investments, personal expenditures, and necessary necessities. Financial objectives might easily be subordinated to urgent purchases in the absence of a strategy. When making daily decisions, a budget makes future priorities more apparent. Spending decisions can be more carefully considered, for instance, when an individual is aware that a specific sum is set aside each month for a significant objective. Thus, budgeting turns financial objectives from concepts into regular activities.

Because automation eliminates the requirement for pure willpower, it can facilitate the achievement of goals. Shortly after revenue is received, automatic transfers can send funds from a primary account to an investment or savings account. This strategy can help guarantee that savings occur regularly before funds are spent on less crucial items. Although automation can foster a beneficial habit, it cannot completely replace the requirement for financial literacy. Repeated contributions can add up over time and show improvement. When contributions are made regularly over an extended period of time, even modest amounts can gain significance.

Another crucial component of successful goal-setting is monitoring progress. Improving something that is never measured is difficult. The effectiveness of the current plan can be determined by looking at savings balances, debt amounts, investment contributions, or progress toward large purchases. Because financial progress is apparent, tracking can also serve as a source of inspiration. The person can determine the cause and make changes if progress is slower than anticipated. Maybe income has changed, spending has gone up, or the initial goal was not achievable. These findings might be viewed as helpful information for refining the plan rather than as failures.

Personal ideals should also be reflected in financial objectives. Money is a tool, and various people use it to promote their own ideas of what constitutes a meaningful existence. Education may be important to some, home ownership may be important to others, starting a business may be important to others, and future independence or family support may be more important to yet others. There isn't a set of financial objectives that everyone has to adhere to. It's crucial to determine what matters to you personally and then make deliberate use of funds to support those objectives. Since they offer a compelling justification for today's sacrifices, goals that are rooted in true values are frequently simpler to uphold.

Differentiating between aims and wants is also crucial. Wanting something might spur enthusiasm right away, but achieving a financial goal takes preparation and dedication. A person may desire a car, a new gadget, or a costly vacation, but making such a purchase without taking debt and savings into account can hinder long-term success. Making a want a goal requires weighing its cost, assessing whether it aligns with current objectives, and figuring out how to appropriately pay for it. This strategy does not imply that enjoyment should be avoided. It entails ensuring that satisfaction in the near term does not continuously compromise significant long-term goals.

When establishing financial goals, unforeseen changes should also be taken into account. Family obligations may arise, income may rise or fall, expenses may alter, or new difficulties may arise due to the state of the economy. An unadaptable financial strategy could prove challenging to stick to. Goals should therefore be reviewed on a regular basis. It's not always a sign of surrender to change a deadline or contribution amount. It can just be a reflection of a shift in the situation. With a resilient strategy, objectives can change while maintaining their overarching purpose. Being adaptable helps stop short-term setbacks from becoming long-term abandonment of financial advancement.

Long-term financial objectives are particularly beneficial because they inspire young folks to look beyond the present. Although retirement may seem far off, starting early can give investments and savings more time to increase potentially. Similarly, it may take years of planning to start a business, buy real estate, or become financially independent. Since significant financial gains never occur overnight, long-term objectives promote patience. They also assist people in appreciating the significance of regular little deeds. Regular contributions over a long period of time can have a bigger effect than sporadic, large-scale, hard-to-maintain initiatives.

In the end, establishing financial objectives is about giving money management direction, discipline, and purpose. A person may decide what to save for, how much to set aside, which costs should be prioritized, and what financial habits need to be altered with the aid of clear goals. Goals that are effective are time-based, precise, quantifiable, practical, and linked to personal values. Budgeting, regular savings, careful spending, progress monitoring, and evaluation should all be used to help them. Early financial goal-setting can have advantages for young adults that go well beyond any one purchase or savings objective. It can foster an attitude where money is seen as a resource that can be purposefully allocated toward independence, security, opportunity, and significant future accomplishments. Every choice becomes a part of a bigger strategy for creating a stable and meaningful financial life when financial objectives are well-defined and consistently pursued.

Preparing Major Milestones

As significant life events frequently involve large expenses, new responsibilities, and decisions that can affect financial stability for many years, preparing for major milestones requires careful financial planning. Many people go through significant life changes during their early adult years, such as finishing school, beginning a career, moving into a house, buying a car, getting married, providing for family members, launching a business, or getting ready for long-term financial independence. These achievements can be thrilling and fulfilling, but if they are not planned for, they can also become financially stressful. A person has more time to save, weigh options, control risks, and make decisions without undue financial pressure when they are able to anticipate future needs.

Clearly defining the objective is the first step in getting ready for a significant milestone. Without a specific goal, it is challenging to plan for a general desire like wanting to buy a house or become financially independent. A more precise objective could be figuring out what kind of house is affordable, how much money will be required for upfront expenses, and when the purchase could actually take place. In a similar vein, someone who intends to pursue further education can budget for living expenses, tuition, supplies, transportation, and other costs. By defining the milestone, an abstract concept becomes a measurable financial goal that can be modified over time.

It is equally important to estimate the total cost of a milestone. People frequently overlook smaller expenses that can add up in favor of concentrating on the biggest expense. For instance, buying a car entails more than just the purchase price. The overall cost may be impacted by insurance, registration, maintenance, fuel, repairs, and financing. In addition to closing costs, utilities, maintenance, property taxes, insurance, and repairs, a home may need a down payment. The costs of healthcare, childcare, education, food, clothing, and transportation can all increase when you start a family. A person can prepare for the ongoing financial obligations related to a significant decision by taking the entire cost into account.

A key component of effective preparation is time. A person can break up a big financial goal into smaller contributions if they start saving early. Waiting until a milestone is near can put undue strain on you and necessitate much larger monthly savings. Additionally, early planning allows for greater flexibility in the event that circumstances change. More time gives you the chance to modify the plan if your income temporarily declines or the goal's cost goes up. Therefore, it is beneficial to start early because time gives you more options rather than because the future can be perfectly predicted.

Managing significant goals can be made simpler with a dedicated savings plan. Money meant for one milestone may not be spent on unrelated purchases if it is separated according to its intended use. A person can set a specific goal and make consistent contributions if they are saving for a business, a house, a car, or education. By transferring funds into savings on a regular basis, automatic transfers can facilitate the process. This method helps make preparation a regular financial habit and lessens reliance on motivation.

The plan should continue to include emergency savings as a key component. When someone is getting ready to reach a significant milestone, they might be tempted to use every peso they have, but unforeseen costs can happen at any time. A well-thought-out savings plan may be hampered by medical expenses, urgent repairs, temporary income loss, family obligations, or other emergencies. Keeping an emergency fund lowers the possibility that milestone savings will need to be used for unforeseen issues and offers protection. Additionally, it can lessen the need for costly borrowing.

Another crucial factor is debt management. Sometimes borrowing is necessary to reach significant milestones, especially when it comes to education, real estate, cars, or business endeavors. When the expenses are reasonable, and the goal aligns with a sensible long-term plan, borrowing can be beneficial. Excessive debt, however, can limit one's flexibility in the future. The interest rate, total cost of repayment, monthly payment, repayment period, and impact on other financial objectives should all be taken into account before taking out a loan. A milestone should enhance a person's life without imposing unmanageable financial obligations.

Growth in income can increase the likelihood of reaching milestones. By acquiring practical skills, gaining experience, going back to school, enhancing their professional credentials, or locating other sources of income, young adults can increase their financial capacity. Progress can be accelerated when earnings rise by allocating a portion of the extra funds to significant objectives. This is especially beneficial because raising income can increase financial capacity without necessitating cost reductions for every improvement. Controlled spending and intentional efforts to boost earning potential are frequently combined in a sound financial plan.

It is also necessary to comprehend opportunity costs in order to prepare for milestones. Typically, funds allocated for one purpose cannot be used concurrently for another. Investing, debt repayment, and other savings objectives may be postponed by a big purchase. This does not imply that big purchases should always be avoided. Rather, one should think about what they are gaining and what other opportunities might be missed. Considering these trade-offs promotes more deliberate choices and lessens the possibility of making costly commitments based only on immediate thrills.

Since life rarely follows a precise financial plan, flexibility is another crucial component of preparation. A person might relocate, experience a shift in family responsibilities, change careers, put off a purchase, or find a new opportunity. A solid plan should be adaptable. Extending the deadline, raising revenue, lowering the target cost, or changing other financial priorities could be the answer if a goal starts to seem less achievable.

Modifying a plan is not a sign of failure. It shows that one can react to new information with intelligence.

Relationships and family obligations can also be impacted by significant life events. Open communication may be necessary when making decisions about marriage, children, shared property, or financial support. Expectations regarding spending, saving, debt, housing, education, and family responsibilities can vary from person to person. Cooperation can be enhanced, and misunderstandings can be avoided by talking about these issues before making significant commitments. When all parties involved in the decision are aware of the expenses, obligations, and long-term consequences, financial preparation is more successful.

Maintaining realistic milestone preparation is facilitated by regular progress reviews. One can review income and expenses, assess whether the original timeline is still feasible, and compare current savings with the target amount. Adjustments can be made before the milestone becomes urgent if progress is slower than anticipated. Consider increasing contributions, cutting back on wasteful spending, looking for other sources of income, or extending the deadline. Evaluating progress also makes it possible to identify gains and sustain motivation.

In the end, preparing for significant milestones teaches valuable financial habits that go beyond any one objective. Planning ahead, estimating expenses, saving consistently, managing risk, controlling debt, increasing income, and adapting to changing conditions are all skills that it fosters. Because financial responsibilities are constantly changing, these skills can be used repeatedly throughout life. The planning process is still helpful even if the milestone itself changes.

A person who is well-prepared does not necessarily know everything about the future. Rather, that individual has established a sufficient financial framework to address upcoming opportunities and obligations confidently. Major milestone preparation entails realizing that significant accomplishments frequently call for resources well in advance of the event. Major transitions can be made easier for young adults by setting clear goals, estimating total costs, starting early, keeping emergency savings, carefully managing debt, increasing earning potential, and routinely reviewing progress. The outcome is not just the capacity to pay for a specific event but also the growth of a more solid financial base that facilitates increased freedom, adaptability, and self-assurance throughout life's various phases.

Reviewing Financial Progress

Since planning is not the only way to achieve financial success, reviewing financial progress is a crucial habit. It can be challenging to determine whether a person's budget, savings objectives, debt reduction, and investment initiatives are truly yielding the anticipated results if the results aren't routinely monitored. Examining financial development is taking the time to look at earnings, outlays, debt, savings, investments, and advancement toward personal objectives. It is not about labeling every financial choice as either good or negative. Rather, it is a process of taking lessons from present outcomes and adjusting as needed. Early adoption of this practice can help young adults become more conscious, disciplined, and self-assured while also making it simpler for them to adapt to changes in their long-term priorities, income, spending, and obligations.

Examining whether actual expenditure aligns with the financial plan is among the first things to do. When a budget is created, it may appear logical, but actual circumstances may differ. Spending can go beyond budget due to unexpected purchases, household bills, entertainment, transportation, food costs, and subscriptions. These discrepancies can be found by routinely reviewing spending. A person may find that certain expenses have escalated over time or that a number of minor transactions are costing more than anticipated. This information offers a chance to make changes before spending issues worsen. The goal is to understand where money is going and whether spending matches current objectives, rather than to eliminate every pleasure expense.

Regular reviews of savings progress are also necessary. When you have a defined goal and a mechanism to track your progress, saving money is easy. A person may have objectives for future requirements such as schooling, a home, a business, travel, or emergency funds. It is possible to determine whether the present contribution rate is adequate by comparing the amount saved to the desired goal. A number of measures could be taken into consideration if the pace of improvement is slower than anticipated. Increasing savings, cutting back on wasteful spending, extending the time frame, or finding ways to boost revenue are all possible options. If development proceeds more quickly than anticipated, the extra momentum could present a chance to bolster another financial priority. Saving becomes a quantifiable process when it is reviewed on a regular basis.

Because debt has a significant impact on future financial flexibility, it should be given special consideration. Examining outstanding balances, interest expenses, necessary payments, and the rate at which balances are decreasing are all part of reviewing debt progress. A person may need to look into interest costs or borrowing patterns if they regularly make payments but see little decrease in their debt. Income that may be put toward investments and savings can be consumed by high-cost debt. Because each payment can be seen as a step toward greater financial freedom, tracking debt reduction can also serve as a source of motivation. Observing the balance decrease over time makes progress concrete and emphasizes the importance of sound financial practices.

Another area that can profit from regular evaluation is credit management. Access to financial products, housing, loans, and other opportunities can be impacted by credit. Examining credit data can reveal mistakes, late payments, excessive borrowing, or other problems that could require attention. Understanding the terms of credit agreements, managing borrowing, and making timely payments are all components of responsible credit use. Regular credit assessments can help a young adult understand how their financial actions impact their future prospects. Consistent attention is more beneficial than trying to repair everything at once because building healthy credit is typically a protracted process.

Investment development should also be assessed, but it's crucial to refrain from examining investments so often that transient market fluctuations cause needless anxiety. When reviewing investments, the major focus should be on whether the overall strategy is still suitable for the individual's objectives, time horizon, risk tolerance, and financial situation. Market prices are subject to fluctuations, and the effectiveness of a long-term plan is not always indicated by short-term results. A young investor should think about whether contributions are continuing as scheduled, whether expenses are acceptable, and whether the portfolio is still suitably diversified. Without promoting emotional responses to typical market swings, periodic review can assist in identifying changes that actually need attention.

Another crucial component of financial advancement is income. A person's financial status can be improved by both cutting costs and raising earning potential. Analyzing income over time can show whether attempts to advance one's profession, gain new skills, take on more jobs, or do other things are yielding significant outcomes. A young adult may find that their earning potential is boosted by obtaining a qualification, honing their professional abilities, switching jobs, negotiating pay, or creating a second source of income. Continued investment in career development may be encouraged by this information. Income stagnation may also indicate the need to look for new possibilities or acquire more marketable skills.

Both numbers and conduct should be considered when evaluating financial progress. Daily routines frequently have an impact on financial outcomes. Frequent impulsive buys, emotional buying, erratic budgeting, or a propensity to use credit for needless expenses can all make it difficult for someone to save money. Examining the final account balance alone may not always be as helpful as identifying these tendencies. It is simpler to think about a workable modification once a behavior has been identified. For instance, automatic savings could be advantageous for someone who usually spends money right away after getting paid. Recurring charges may be reviewed by someone who frequently overspends on subscriptions. Therefore, the goal of financial review is not only to quantify results but also to comprehend the actions that lead to those results.

Additionally, financial advancement should be evaluated in relation to one's own objectives rather than the financial circumstances of others. Social media can give the appearance that everyone else is making more money, investing more, traveling more, or buying more expensive goods. Comparing one's own development to these outward manifestations can put undue pressure on oneself and result in bad choices. Comparing one's present financial situation with one's past performance is more beneficial. Significant progress has been made if debt is lower than it was the previous year, savings are higher, spending is more restrained, or income has increased. Instead of focusing on outward appearances, financial success should be evaluated based on personal goals and circumstances.

Frequent financial evaluations can also show whether objectives need to be adjusted. Life is not always the same. A young adult may start a new career, relocate, take on family obligations, pursue further education, launch a business, or establish new long-term goals. A goal that made sense a few years ago might not be the most crucial one now. Examining finances offers a chance to reevaluate priorities and ensure that funds are still allocated to the most important things. A goal change does not equate to failure. When the transformation represents a real change in circumstances or values, it might show maturity and insight.

Honesty and practicality are key components of an effective financial evaluation. Financial issues do not go away by avoiding hard numbers. The first step to improvement is identifying the issue, whether it be excessive spending, mounting debt, or inadequate savings. Finding what can be managed should be the main goal of the review. While spending choices, saving practices, debt repayment, and financial literacy can frequently be enhanced, income may not always be readily adjustable and unforeseen costs cannot always be avoided. Financial difficulties can seem more doable when they are divided into smaller tasks.

A significant psychological advantage can also be obtained by reviewing progress. When one is focused on long-term objectives, financial management might occasionally feel like a never-ending sequence of sacrifices. A young adult might be reminded that regular behaviors are yielding results by looking back at their progress. Disciplined habits can be demonstrated by an increased emergency fund, a decreasing debt load, an increase in retirement savings, or an increase in income. Reasonable milestones can be celebrated to reward good conduct without promoting wasteful spending. Instead of just being a set of numbers, progress becomes a source of inspiration.

In the end, evaluating financial progress is an ongoing process of assessment, education, and modification. It aids in determining whether expenditure and income are still in balance, whether savings objectives are being met, whether debt is getting easier to handle, whether investments are still suitable, and whether financial behavior supports long-term aspirations. The goal is to raise awareness and promote progress rather than perfection. Making regular financial evaluations a habit can help young adults identify chances for stronger financial progress and stop minor issues from growing into bigger ones. Money becomes simpler to comprehend and manage when financial progress is evaluated honestly and regularly. Every evaluation offers helpful facts that can direct the subsequent choice, assisting an individual in gaining more stability, self-assurance, adaptability, and financial future control.

Designing Your Financial Roadmap

Decisions that might otherwise seem unrelated to one another are guided by a financial roadmap. New responsibilities, shifting income, educational costs, transportation costs, family expectations, lifestyle choices, and financially demanding opportunities are all common aspects of young adulthood. It is simple to make financial decisions based solely on what seems urgent right now when one lacks a clear sense of direction. By linking current decisions with future priorities, a roadmap modifies that pattern. It assists in turning money from something that is merely earned and spent into a resource that can be purposefully managed. Making an ideal plan is not what makes this process so important. It results from learning to make deliberate choices even when conditions change. When used regularly, financial planning can boost self-esteem, lessen needless stress, increase readiness, and make significant objectives seem attainable. Financial decisions can become reactive if they are disregarded. Because spending grows more quickly than progress, a person may make more money but still feel stuck financially. Long-term objectives may consistently be put off, bills may only be paid when they become urgent, and savings may continue to fluctuate. Therefore, having a roadmap has a far greater practical impact than having a written budget. It affects decisions about housing, careers, relationships, educational opportunities, emergencies, significant purchases, and the flexibility to change course when conditions change.

By the end of this chapter, you will be able to make a workable financial plan that links your present income and resources with significant short-term and long-term goals, determine which financial actions should be prioritized based on your unique situation, and modify your plan in response to changes in income, expenses, obligations, or opportunities without giving up on your overall financial direction. These results are intended to transform planning from a concept into a recurring action. The objective is not just to understand what financial planning entails, but to apply that understanding when making decisions about what to do with the money that is currently available. A helpful roadmap should indicate what needs to be addressed immediately, what can wait, what requires ongoing observation, and what future outcomes your present decisions are promoting.

Imagine a young worker who wants to move into a better apartment in two years and has a steady monthly income. Rather than merely hoping to save enough, the individual assesses current monthly expenses, calculates the amount that can be saved each month, estimates the amount required for an emergency reserve, and identifies the anticipated moving costs. The plan may show that money that could be used to support the housing goal is being spent on certain convenience purchases. Every enjoyable expense does not have to be eliminated. Rather, spending is rearranged to prioritize funding. While automatic transfers ensure consistent progress, a different savings account can be utilized for the moving goal. The individual evaluates income and expenses every few months and modifies the savings amount as needed. The key takeaway is that by turning the objective into concrete financial actions, it becomes manageable.

The same idea is demonstrated in a short story. Consider Daniel, a young worker who gets his first steady pay check. At first, he feels financially successful because he can afford more than he could while he was in school. He starts to spend freely, upgrading electronics, placing frequent food orders, and accepting all social invitations. Very little is left at the end of each month. He has to borrow money from a friend due to an unforeseen expense. Daniel understands that his income is not the only issue he faces. He has never made up his mind about what he wants his money to do. He starts allocating his income before spending it, creates a small emergency fund, cuts back on purchases that don't align with his priorities, and establishes a long-term savings goal. Even though his financial circumstances are not ideal, a year later, he has something more valuable than a bigger bank account. He is in charge of his choices. He can react to another unforeseen expense without resorting to debt right away. His roadmap has altered not just how much money he saves but also how he thinks.

Considering your financial roadmap as a navigation system is a helpful metaphor. Traffic, road construction, unforeseen detours, and destination changes cannot be avoided by a navigation system. Rather, it provides guidance and aids in adapting to changing circumstances. The same is true of your financial life. Your income might fluctuate, an emergency might arise, a job opportunity might necessitate moving, or a significant expense might show up sooner than anticipated. Your financial plan has not failed because of these occurrences. They indicate that the route must be changed. A person who lacks financial direction might respond to every change by choosing an entirely different course of action. When someone has a roadmap, they can make changes without losing sight of their destination.

The Direction and Action Method is a straightforward framework that can be used for immediate application. Determine the destination first. Put down the three financial outcomes—building an emergency fund, paying off high-cost debt, buying a house, financing education, launching a business, or getting ready for retirement—that would significantly improve the next few years. Next, decide where to begin. Without passing judgment on yourself, examine your present income, necessary expenses, debts, savings, and available financial resources. A realistic foundation is produced by accurate information. Next, determine the difference between your current situation and your desired future state. Instead of depending on hope, figure out what needs to change if you want to accumulate a sizable savings balance but currently have little. Next, decide what needs to be done to close the gap. These could include cutting back on wasteful spending, boosting income, automating savings, making more aggressive debt payments, or rerouting future raises toward crucial objectives. Set a deadline after that. Give each major priority a realistic target date because a goal without a deadline can be put off indefinitely. Lastly, review and reroute. Examine what worked, what didn't, and what needs to be adjusted once a month. The review's objective is not self-criticism. It serves to maintain the roadmap's relevance to reality.

When competing financial priorities arise, this process becomes extremely valuable. In addition to continuing their education, a young adult may wish to support their family, travel, buy a car, invest, and keep an emergency fund. Every decision involves trade-offs due to limited income. These trade-offs are visible on a roadmap. Consider whether a purchase advances your chosen course rather than just whether it is reasonably priced. Technically, a purchase might be within this month's budget, but it would still postpone a crucial future goal. Similarly, if spending money on something worthwhile has been purposefully incorporated into the plan, it is not inherently reckless. Making deliberate trade-offs instead of categorizing every expense as either good or bad leads to financial maturity.

Additionally, flexibility should be protected in the roadmap. Seldom does life have a clear financial trajectory. Unemployment, an unexpected opportunity, family obligations, moving, or a shift in priorities can all happen to an individual. Including flexibility in a plan entails maintaining a certain amount of savings, avoiding obligations that will deplete future earnings, and reevaluating objectives as conditions change. Because it views every deviation as a failure, a strict plan can become demoralizing. A flexible roadmap acknowledges that sometimes it's necessary to slow down one objective while safeguarding another. The secret is to make intentional changes instead of letting events dictate every financial choice.

Distinguishing between financial urgency and financial importance is another crucial application. Not all urgent issues contribute to long-term stability, but urgent matters require immediate attention. While retirement savings might be crucial, a late bill might be urgent. A big purchase might need careful consideration, but a sudden sale might feel urgent. It is possible to stop short-term pressure from using up all available resources by learning to differentiate between these categories. Important priorities are given a spot in the plan before they become emergencies thanks to a solid roadmap.

The fact that financial planning produces proof of advancement is its deeper value. It can be challenging to see progress when your goals are just in your head. You can observe changes over time when you monitor savings, debt reduction, investment contributions, emergency reserves, and income growth. Every action you complete shows that your decisions are having an impact, so even little progress can boost your confidence. This self-assurance may inspire wiser choices in other spheres of life.

Planning should be transformed into individual action through reflection. Which financial objective would have the biggest positive impact on your life over the coming years? Which present spending pattern is subtly diverting funds from a higher priority? How much money could you actually put toward your top priority each month? What kind of financial setback might interfere with your present plans, and how can you be ready for it before it occurs? What financial action can you take this week to get closer to your desired future?

Only when a roadmap is put to use does it become beneficial. Setting goals is just the first step; the true value comes when those goals impact day-to-day choices. The best strategy isn't always difficult. It is practical enough to be used frequently, adaptable enough to withstand change, and clear enough to direct decisions. Thousands of decisions, many of which are commonplace and simple to ignore, will influence your financial future. Your path can be strengthened by each choice you make to invest before lifestyle inflation takes over, save before spending, prepare before borrowing, or review before committing.

Rather than waiting for a perfect financial situation, the most crucial step is to start with the information and resources that are currently available. To make a better path, you don't need a lot of money, total assurance, or an impeccable past. You must be willing to act consistently, be honest about where you are, and have a clear idea of where you want to go. A financial roadmap transforms long-term objectives into current obligations and current obligations into quantifiable advancements. It can offer stability in times of uncertainty and confidence in times of opportunity when reviewed on a regular basis. A single financial choice does not control the future. It is constructed by making repeated choices that progressively increase the realism, achievability, and security of your intended course.

CHAPTER X

Creating Lasting Financial Success

Building Financial Discipline

One of the most crucial abilities a young adult may acquire is developing financial discipline because a person's ability to manage their money consistently is just as significant to their financial success as their earnings. Making deliberate choices about earning, spending, saving, investing, and borrowing even when there are simpler or more instantly pleasurable options available is known as financial discipline. It is the capacity to balance current demands with future financial security. A disciplined individual does not have to live a terribly constrained lifestyle or abstain from all pleasures. Rather, financial discipline entails knowing one's own boundaries, identifying objectives, and developing long-term goal-supporting behaviors.

Awareness is the first step towards financial discipline. Without understanding where money comes from and goes, it is impossible to handle it properly. A better understanding of financial behavior can be obtained by keeping track of income and expenses, which can also highlight trends that might otherwise go missed. Even though small expenditures might seem innocuous on their own, recurring expenses can add up to a sizeable amount of monthly cash. A young adult can identify which expenses are essential, which offer significant value, and which can be cut by recognizing these patterns. Awareness generates the knowledge required to make wiser decisions.

Another crucial component of financial discipline is making and adhering to a reasonable budget. Before money is spent, a budget provides it a purpose. Savings, debt repayment, investments, and discretionary expenditure should come after essential expenses. A sound budget should be feasible to stick to over time. A too rigid strategy might be challenging to adhere to, which can result in dissatisfaction or desertion. When the budget provides for some flexibility for fair enjoyment and matches actual circumstances, financial discipline is more successful. Consistency, not perfection, is the aim.

Another effective financial habit is to learn to postpone needless purchases. Digital buying and contemporary advertising make it simple to spend money right away. It's possible for someone to buy something they find appealing online without thinking about whether they really need it. Waiting a while before making non-essential purchases can help cut down on impulsive expenditures. During this time, the buyer can think about whether the purchase advances a significant objective, whether the product is reasonably priced, and whether the funds could be better spent elsewhere. Although it may seem challenging at first, delaying pleasure can greatly enhance financial control and get easier with practice.

Discipline is also necessary for constant saving. Waiting to save what's left over after spending frequently leads to very little being saved. Treating saving as a deliberate financial obligation is a more effective strategy. Savings can become more automatic if funds are set aside as soon as income is received. This practice can eventually generate funds for significant future objectives as well as emergency reserves. Regular contributions can create a habit that is easier to sustain when income rises, even if the amount saved is small. Often, the habit is more significant than the initial quantity.

Using credit responsibly is another aspect of financial discipline. Although borrowing creates future commitments, credit can be convenient and helpful with some purchases. Growing balances and costly interest rates might result from using credit without taking repayment capacity into account. A disciplined borrower evaluates if a purchase is actually necessary and is aware of the whole cost of borrowing. Avoiding needless debt, managing balances, and making timely bill payments can prevent future income from being depleted by past expenditures. Instead of being viewed as an extension of income, credit should be viewed as a financial obligation.

Learning to differentiate necessities from wants is another aspect of developing financial discipline. While wants include numerous optional purchases that increase comfort or enjoyment, needs often include necessities such as basic housing, food, transportation, utilities, and required healthcare. Due to individual differences in circumstances, the distinction is not always entirely straightforward. Spending decisions can be improved, though, by routinely determining whether a purchase is necessary, valuable, or merely transient. This does not imply doing away with desires. It entails ensuring that desires don't constantly conflict with crucial financial priorities.

Maintaining progress at times of low motivation is another crucial aspect of discipline. It can take months or years to reach financial objectives, and excitement eventually wanes. A person may start a savings plan with great enthusiasm, but after a few months, they may lose interest. Even when motivation wanes, sound financial practices persist. The amount of willpower needed can be decreased by automatic saves, planned bill payments, spending caps, and frequent financial evaluations. Relying just on incentives is frequently less dependable than using systems.

Regular evaluation and correction should be part of financial discipline. It is not necessary for a financial strategy to be the same throughout life. Goals, obligations, income, and expenses are all subject to change. A person might get promoted, relocate, start helping family members, buy a house, or have their income unexpectedly cut. It is possible to make changes before minor issues turn into major ones by reviewing the budget and financial objectives. Being adaptable is not a sign of weakness. It is crucial to uphold discipline in situations that change.

Patience is also necessary to develop financial discipline. Many financial advancements are slow and might not show noticeable effects right away. One contribution at a time, an emergency fund expands. One payment at a time, debt lowers. Long-term engagement and recurring donations help investments develop. It's crucial to pay attention to the direction of financial movement rather than anticipating rapid change because improvement can be gradual. Small activities can add up to significant outcomes when they are consistent.

Developing a trustworthy relationship with money is the ultimate goal of financial discipline. It entails making decisions that support long-term objectives, borrowing sensibly, investing carefully, saving regularly, and spending purposefully. Early adoption of these practices by young individuals can lay a solid foundation for financial independence. Being flawless or never making mistakes are not prerequisites for discipline. Everyone has moments of excess, unforeseen costs, or financial difficulties. It's important to acknowledge errors, grow from them, and resume responsible behavior. Financial discipline might eventually become less of a challenge and more of an organic approach to money management. Benefits that stretch well beyond a single budget can be obtained by maintaining consistency, prioritizing key objectives, and controlling spending. It can boost a person's financial confidence, lessen needless stress, and grant them more autonomy to make significant life decisions based on possibilities and ideals rather than financial pressure.

Achieving Financial Independence

Reaching a point where one can handle daily necessities and significant life choices without being totally reliant on another person or a single source of income is known as financial independence. Being financially independent for a young adult involves more than just accumulating wealth. It involves gaining sufficient financial security, resources, abilities, and self-assurance to make decisions based on personal priorities rather than ongoing financial strain. It can entail being able to manage debt responsibly, save regularly, invest for the future, pay regular expenses, deal with emergencies, and make important decisions without heavily depending on family members or taking on excessive debt. Rather than a single, spectacular financial success, the path to independence typically develops gradually through numerous pragmatic habits.

Gaining control over daily expenses is one of the first steps to financial independence. If income routinely vanishes without a clear understanding of where it goes, a person cannot achieve long-term independence. Identifying necessary expenses, flexible spending, savings, debt repayment, and future investments is made easier with the creation of a realistic spending plan. The goal of a spending plan is to ensure that present expenditures do not continuously obstruct future objectives, not to take away enjoyment from life. Understanding the difference between needs and wants is especially crucial because many financial problems start when discretionary purchases turn into regular obligations. Intentional spending allows for the allocation of more income toward the development of financial security.

Another crucial foundation is provided by emergency savings. The capacity to manage unforeseen circumstances without immediately resorting to costly debt or depending on others for assistance is necessary for financial independence. Unexpected repairs, brief income disruptions, urgent expenses, and other financial difficulties can all be covered by an emergency fund. The right amount depends on individual circumstances, but it's crucial to accumulate savings and have emergency funds on hand regularly. Because an unforeseen expense becomes a manageable issue rather than an urgent crisis, having this reserve can boost confidence.

Reducing detrimental debt is also crucial. While excessive high-interest debt can restrict financial freedom, it can be beneficial when it serves a significant and controllable purpose. The amount of money available for investments, savings, professional advancement, and personal objectives is decreased by large monthly payments. Financial flexibility gradually increases when costly debt is paid off because less money is spent on previous purchases. A young adult is more likely to become independent if they learn how to borrow responsibly, comprehend interest rates, and make regular payments. Paying off current debt is frequently just as important as avoiding needless debt.

Another important component of becoming independent is improving one's earning capacity. While developing useful skills can eventually increase income, controlling expenses has its limits. Career opportunities can be enhanced by education, professional training, technical proficiency, communication skills, leadership experience, and specialized knowledge. Instead of concentrating solely on reducing expenses, a young adult should view income growth as a crucial financial objective. Increasing one's professional worth may open doors to better pay, career advancement, better jobs, or extra revenue. Increased earning potential facilitates investing, saving, handling emergencies, and pursuing long-term objectives.

Independence can also be strengthened by establishing several sources of funding. While having multiple jobs is not always necessary, expanding one's sources of income can lessen reliance on a single employer or salary. Additional flexibility may be offered by freelancing, consulting, small business ventures, creative work, or other revenue-generating endeavors. On the other hand, extra revenue must be carefully and sustainably developed. The goal is to progressively build resources that offer more financial options rather than to exhaust oneself by working nonstop.

Another crucial component of long-term independence is investing. While investments can present chances for long-term growth, savings offer security and liquidity. A young adult may progressively accumulate assets that can support future financial security if they make wise and regular investments. Investment choices should be grounded in research rather than ephemeral excitement and should take into account individual objectives, risk tolerance, and time horizon. Because investment values can change, patience and diversification are crucial. Financial independence is attained by creating a disciplined strategy that can be sustained over time rather than by trying to forecast every market movement.

Controlling lifestyle inflation is another aspect of financial independence. It can be tempting to immediately increase spending on housing, transportation, entertainment, clothes, technology, and other comforts as income rises. While some lifestyle enhancements make sense, spending every extra dollar earned can stop wealth from increasing. By allocating a portion of each income increase to savings, investments, debt reduction, or other worthwhile financial objectives, an individual can enhance their independence. This strikes a balance between building more freedom for the future and enjoying a higher income now.

Having specific long-term objectives is another crucial component. Different people have different definitions of financial independence. One person might be able to live debt-free. For another, it might entail starting a business, owning a house, retiring early, providing for a family, or having sufficient investments to pay for future needs. Determining how much money and which financial resources are required is made simpler when one defines independence for themselves. Then, objectives can be divided into more manageable benchmarks that can be assessed and evaluated. This gives the impression that a distant goal is more attainable.

In the end, becoming financially independent is a gradual process that requires making disciplined decisions. Spending awareness, emergency preparedness, responsible debt management, income development, regular saving, sensible investing, and deliberate goal-setting are all necessary. Additionally, it takes time because significant financial independence seldom happens overnight. Even though a young adult may start out with little money and resources, over time, consistent habits can lead to substantial advancements. Financial independence can be strengthened by managing emergency expenses without incurring new debt, reducing debt, developing new skills, saving money, and making investments. Having more money is not the biggest advantage. It is giving people more control over their decisions and lessening the worry that one unforeseen circumstance might totally ruin financial plans. A person can progressively establish a financial position that supports freedom, stability, opportunity, and increased confidence in the future by developing sound financial habits early in life and honing them throughout.

Creating A Lasting Legacy

Thinking beyond short-term financial success and taking into account how decisions made today may affect other people and future generations is essential to leaving a lasting legacy. The quantity of money a person leaves behind is not the only aspect of their legacy. Values, knowledge, connections, chances, prudent financial practices, charitable contributions, businesses, real estate, investments, and teachings that continue to help others can all be included. Young adults frequently have a lot of urgent commitments, so considering legacy may seem premature. However, forming the correct habits at a young age can lay the groundwork for financial resources and moral principles to have a significant impact eventually.

Knowing what is really important is the first step toward creating a strong legacy. Although it can offer possibilities and security, money does not always translate into a fulfilling existence. When making financial decisions, one should think about the values they wish to exhibit. Responsibility, charity, education, independence, hard work, honesty, compassion, or dedication to family are a few examples of these values. Wealth becomes a tool for producing favorable results rather than just a gauge of success when financial decisions are linked to human beliefs. In addition to accumulating more, the goal of resource building is to determine how such resources may support significant individuals, causes, and objectives.

One of the first pillars of a long-lasting legacy is financial stability. When one's own finances are continuously unsteady, it is challenging to offer people significant help. Increased financial resilience can be achieved through developing prudent spending practices, preserving savings, controlling debt, making long-term investments, and safeguarding assets. Effective money management can eventually increase a person's ability to provide for family members, support community initiatives, finance educational opportunities, or have other long-lasting effects. As a result, managing finances responsibly becomes crucial to getting ready to give rather than receive.

Another effective way to leave a legacy is through education. While money can eventually be spent, decisions can be influenced by information for many years. Stronger financial habits can be developed by teaching kids, family, friends, or younger community members about long-term planning, budgeting, investing, saving, and responsibility. It is not necessary to be wealthy to impart valuable knowledge. Giving someone money may not always be as beneficial as acting responsibly and outlining the rationale behind financial decisions. The advantages of passing down financial knowledge from one generation to the next might last long after the initial lesson was imparted.

Creating possibilities for others is another way to leave a lasting legacy. Financial resources can be used to assist community development, education, training, business, housing, or other worthwhile endeavors. Giving someone access to a chance or helping them acquire new skills might have far-reaching consequences. Supporting someone's education, for instance, may increase their earning potential, which may subsequently help their own family. In this sense, careful financial assistance might set off a series of beneficial events that go beyond a single transaction.

Building a legacy requires generosity, but it must be done carefully. Giving without taking into account one's own financial security may not be sustainable and may cause problems for the giver. Establishing a degree of generosity that is within a person's financial means is a more effective strategy. This could entail making consistent philanthropic contributions, supporting community initiatives, assisting family members with particular needs, or lending time and expertise. The amount of money donated is not the sole way to assess generosity. Support that is consistent and aligns with one's ideals can have a profound impact.

Creating useful assets is another way to leave a lasting impact. Even if the original owner is no longer actively involved, investments, real estate, companies, intellectual property, and other valuable resources may continue to produce advantages. But creating these assets calls for careful preparation and administration. Asset-based legacies should also take into account maintenance expenses, ownership agreements, taxes, legal obligations, and potential beneficiaries or managers. Assets can become sources of conflict or financial hardship rather than opportunities if they are not properly planned.

Ensuring that accumulated assets are transmitted in accordance with an individual's objectives can be facilitated by estate planning. This may entail creating a will, naming beneficiaries, keeping track of crucial financial data, setting up suitable ownership arrangements, and, if needed, obtaining expert legal counsel. Estate planning is not limited to the very rich. Considering what should happen to their property and bank accounts in the future might be beneficial for anyone with significant assets or family responsibilities. Having a clear plan will help loved ones go through challenging times and avoid uncertainty.

When leaving a lasting legacy, family contact is also crucial. When expectations are not communicated honestly, financial issues can occasionally become sources of miscommunication. Greater understanding can be achieved by discussing values, duties, financial objectives, and future plans with family members. These discussions don't always have to center on a person's financial situation. They can concentrate on the guiding concepts of financial choices and the obligations associated with obtaining or handling resources. Future generations can benefit from clear communication about the benefits and responsibilities that come with prosperity.

Additionally, meaningful labor and business can leave a legacy. Establishing a profitable company may help communities, create jobs, service clients, and open doors for future generations. When a business is based on practical products, ethical behavior, and long-term planning, even a little business may make a difference. A family's financial history may include a business that is subsequently passed down to a subsequent generation. But more than just financial success is needed to leave a lasting legacy for your company. It necessitates creating procedures, moral principles, leadership abilities, and knowledge that can be used by others.

Preserving the ideals that go along with financial resources is another crucial aspect of legacy. Dependency, disagreement, or bad decision-making can occasionally result from wealth without responsibility. Future generations can learn how money works and the importance of making good decisions from their parents and other mentors. Giving someone resources may not always be as valuable as teaching them how to handle them. Ideally, a lasting legacy should offer both opportunity and the information needed to make the most of it.

One of the most durable kinds of legacy is probably personal character. People may eventually forget how much money someone has amassed, but they may remember how they treated others, fulfilled obligations, overcame challenges, and improved the lives of others around them. A legacy can be sustained by financial success, but character is what gives it significance. Even in situations where no financial assets are transmitted, future generations can be impacted by acting honorably, honoring agreements, treating others fairly, and using resources properly.

It is also necessary to consider sustainability in order to leave a lasting legacy. Plans that solely rely on consistent high income or unrealistic investment returns should be avoided. Resources and commitments that are relatively sustainable throughout time provide the foundation of a sustainable legacy. This could entail keeping costs under control, diversifying assets, safeguarding valuable resources, and making sure that future obligations are recognized. The possibility that the advantages of accumulated wealth will persist rather than swiftly vanish is increased by sustainable planning.

In the end, leaving a lasting legacy entails determining what should be left over after today's financial choices have yielded their outcomes. It's not only about making money. It is about creating stability, gaining knowledge, helping others, safeguarding priceless resources, and imparting significant values to coming generations. By forming sound financial practices now, young folks can start planning for this kind of legacy. Every choice to learn, save, invest, safeguard possessions, help others, and behave ethically can fit within a bigger narrative. A person progressively leaves a lasting legacy by making consistent decisions that align with their core principles. Wealth can be used to create benefits that last much beyond a person's lifetime when it is paired with knowledge, charity, responsibility, and careful planning.

Building Your Lifelong Financial Future

Financial security is not the result of a single wise choice or a single period of high income, so establishing long-term financial success is important. It is developed through routines that adapt to changing circumstances in life. Even though a young adult may start out with little, the choices they make in these formative years can have an impact on their independence, stability, and future opportunities. A stronger foundation is produced by learning to manage income, spending, saving, debt, investing, protection, and financial objectives as interconnected components of a single system. Consistent application of these principles makes future goals more attainable and financial decisions more deliberate. Ignoring them can cause uncontrolled spending, needless debt, inadequate planning, and lack of preparation to make even a growing income disappear.

When unforeseen events arise, the difference in real life becomes apparent. When circumstances change, a person with financial reserves, manageable obligations, useful skills, suitable investments, and well-defined goals typically has more options. Without these underpinnings, a person might be compelled to take out loans, sell assets at a bad time, put off crucial objectives, or rely significantly on others. Therefore, achieving financial success entails more than just accumulating wealth. It entails building a financial position that can sustain daily living, withstand fair setbacks, and offer prospects for the future.

By the end of this chapter, you will be able to create a lifelong financial system that links earning, spending, saving, investing, debt management, and financial protection; modify your financial choices as your goals and income obligations change; and uphold sensible habits that promote increased financial independence at various phases of life. Instead of emphasizing perfection, these results highlight consistency. The idea is to develop routines that you can stick to even when things don't go as planned.

A young worker who gets paid more is a real-world example. The employee allocates a portion of the increase to investments, a portion to debt reduction, and a portion to emergency savings rather than using the full amount for an expensive lifestyle. Money is still utilized to make daily life better. Stronger savings, fewer debts, and expanding assets are the results of the higher income over a number of years. The key takeaway is that increasing income does not guarantee wealth. When greater earning potential is paired with wise financial choices, wealth is created.

This idea is demonstrated in a short story. Daniel, a young employee, thot that once he received a significantly higher salary, he would start to succeed financially. He believed that saving little sums of money was useless, so he spent the majority of his early earnings. He finally made the decision to start with what he had. He kept tabs on his spending, established a small emergency fund, cut back on needless debt, and made regular, reasonable investments. Instead of letting each raise turn into extra spending, he maintained these habits as his income rose. Years later, Daniel came to understand that consistency was the key to his financial success. His initial contributions were modest, but as his wealth and expertise increased, the habit grew.

Considering financial success as gardening is a helpful metaphor. One day of planting does not make a garden healthy. Regular care, suitable resources, protection, tolerance, and adaptation are all necessary. The same is true of financial life. Financial protection protects against certain setbacks, debt management eliminates needless weight, investing can spur growth, saving creates reserves, and income provides resources. Financial issues can develop covertly if these areas are ignored for an extended period of time. The financial system as a whole can strengthen if they are consistently upheld.

The Lifelong Financial Cycle is a straightforward framework that can assist in putting these concepts into practice right away. Start by making money through useful skills and hard work. Next, manage your income by assigning a specific purpose to each portion of your funds. Put money aside for unforeseen expenses. Cut back on costly or needless debt. Invest wisely to build suitable long-term assets. Use appropriate financial safeguards and security measures to protect your financial progress. Lastly, periodically review the entire system and make any necessary adjustments as your situation changes.

Since professional value can affect financial opportunities, the earning stage should continue into adulthood. Industries shift, new opportunities arise, and skills become outdated. Maintaining one's education can expand one's options and boost earning potential. Then, instead of being automatically transformed into more lifestyle expenses, additional income should be used purposefully.

Knowing where your money is going is essential to managing it. Building wealth is not hampered by spending. The issue is unplanned spending. Money can support future objectives while being used for leisure, relationships, education, travel, and personal necessities. Whether spending reflects priorities and whether there are sufficient resources left over for future needs are crucial questions.

Establishing reserves offers defense against common financial setbacks. Although emergencies are unpredictable, being prepared can lessen their financial impact. When an unforeseen expense arises, even a small reserve can provide breathing room. The reserve can be reviewed and modified as income and responsibilities rise.

Another crucial component of long-term success is lowering needless debt. Paying off debt can reduce future earnings and restrict financial options. The money that was previously used for those payments can be redirected toward savings, investments, or other objectives once costly obligations are reduced. As a result, the focus gradually shifts from making up for the past to creating the future.

It takes patience to increase wealth. Clear objectives, a suitable time horizon, and an awareness of risk should all be linked to investing. Predicting every market movement or pursuing rapid profits are not the goals. Establishing a sensible plan that can be sustained over time is the goal. When given enough time, disciplined behavior and consistent contributions can grow in significance.

Preserving advancement is just as crucial. Vulnerability can be decreased through sound financial accounts, cautious handling of personal data, well-organized records, suitable protection, and deliberate decision-making. One reckless financial choice can cause someone to lose a sizable portion of their wealth after years of accumulation. Protection guarantees that resilience supports growth.

Frequent review maintains the system's usefulness. As you grow older, your financial needs will also change. Priorities can be impacted by changes in employment, family obligations, housing choices, education, business prospects, and retirement planning. For this reason, a budget should be adaptable. Periodically assess your progress and make necessary modifications without compromising the long-term stability-promoting tenets.

These concepts can be put into practice with the help of reflection questions. If you practiced it regularly for the next ten years, which financial habit would have the biggest positive impact on your future? Which aspect of your financial life is most in need of immediate attention right now? Instead of letting all the extra money go toward spending, how will you use future income increases to improve your financial situation? As your responsibilities grow, what financial risks should you be ready for? What particular financial action can you start this week that you will be grateful for in the future?

Repeated decisions are the foundation of long-term financial success. It may seem commonplace to save a little money, pay bills on time, acquire a useful skill, make wise investments, avoid pointless purchases, and safeguard financial information; when these behaviors are repeated for years, their significance increases. Creating a flawless financial life is not the aim. The idea is to design a system that will keep you going even in the face of unpredictability.

The plan you make today won't always be the same for your financial future. Goals may change, income may fluctuate, costs may rise, and unanticipated opportunities may present themselves. A robust financial system is able to adjust while maintaining its top priorities. Thus, flexibility is a component of financial strength. You don't have to give up on your destination in order to alter the route.

Start by assessing your current situation. Determine which financial strengths should be preserved and which should be strengthened. Give your money a purpose. Safeguard a portion of your earnings. Cut back on pointless commitments. Gain useful skills. When ready, make the right investments. Evaluate your development on a regular basis.

The most significant accomplishment is not stopping at a single financial milestone. Financial life goes through several phases, each of which offers fresh chances to grow and learn. Early habits can serve as the basis for later increased independence.

Making responsible financial behavior a way of life leads to long-term success. Keep learning, keep adjusting, and keep making choices that will help you in the future. Every well-considered financial decision creates an additional degree of security. These layers can eventually lead to increased confidence, flexibility, security, and freedom.

Your future financial situation will be influenced not only by your income but also by the things you consistently do with it. Build with caution, grow patiently, protect consistently, and evaluate truthfully. Financial success becomes more than just a destination when these routines are incorporated into daily life. Making decisions, securing opportunities, and constructing a future with more control and direction become a lifelong process.

CONCLUSION

Money and Wealth as a Young Adult From the Ground Up: Master Essential Money Skills for Lifelong Financial Success provides a foundation for understanding how daily financial decisions can influence a person's future. Gaining control over income, expenses, savings, debt, credit, and investments boosts self-assurance. Financial success is the result of steady habits that progressively increase stability, freedom, and opportunity rather than a single choice.

The lessons learned along the way show that consciousness and deliberate action are the first steps toward financial advancement. Managing challenging financial circumstances can be facilitated by developing a realistic budget, saving for emergencies, cutting back on needless debt, safeguarding important assets, and making long-term plans. Ignoring these obligations might result in stress, fewer options, and lost chances. Instead, by putting these ideas into practice, people can become more adaptable and respond to changing situations with greater assurance.

The most crucial stage is to start and keep becoming better. When financial information is applied to everyday conduct, it becomes beneficial. A stronger future is the result of every dollar saved, every deliberate purchase, every responsible payment, and every well-thought-out investment. Young individuals can progressively accumulate long-term wealth and financial security if they learn patience and discipline. Repeated decisions form the future, and sound money management gives you the resources you need to make those decisions with assurance, direction, and increased autonomy.

Thank you for buying and reading/ listening to our book. If you found this book useful/ helpful please take a few minutes and leave a review on the platform where you purchased our book. Your feedback matters greatly to us.